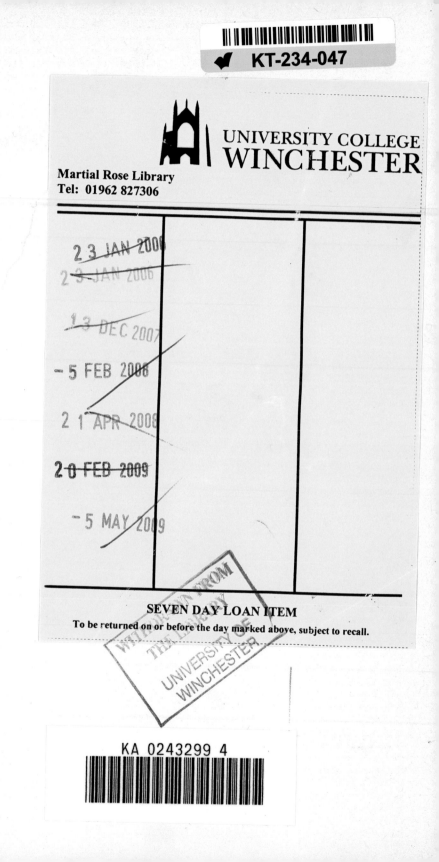

UNIVERSITY COLLEGE
WINCHESTER

SEVEN DAY LOAN ITEM
To be returned on or before the day marked above, subject to recall.

Educating the whole child

Educating the whole child

CROSS-CURRICULAR SKILLS, THEMES AND
DIMENSIONS

EDITED BY
JOHN and IRAM SIRAJ-BLATCHFORD

Open University Press
Buckingham · Philadelphia

Open University Press
Celtic Court
22 Ballmoor
Buckingham
MK18 1XW

and
1900 Frost Road, Suite 101
Bristol, PA 19007, USA

First Published 1995

A catalogue record of this book is available from the British Library

ISBN 0 335 19444 3 (pb)   0 335 19445 1 (hb)

Library of Congress Cataloging-in-Publication Data
Educating the whole child : cross-curricular skills, themes, and
  dimensions / edited by John and Iram Siraj-Blatchford.
      p.   cm.
    Includes bibliographical references and index.
    ISBN 0-335-19445-1. – ISBN 0-335-19444-3 (pbk.)
    1. Education, Elementary–Great Britain–Curricula. 2. Curriculum
  planning–Great Britain. I. Siraj-Blatchford, John. 1952–
  II. Siraj-Blatchford, Iram.
  LB1564.G7E36 1995
  371.19'0941–dc20   94–95443
                                                              CIP

Typeset by Colset Private Ltd, Singapore
Printed in Great Britain by Biddles Ltd, Guildford and King's Lynn

Contents

The editors and contributors

JOHN BENNETT is Health Education Coordinator for Coventry LEA, a post he has held since 1989. Since 1992 he has also had a responsibility for PE as an advisory teacher. Prior to this, John worked in various spheres of education as a secondary teacher, a community worker based in a primary school, a youth worker and a community tutor in a community college. He has been involved in the training of teachers, youth workers and support staff as well as working with parent groups. In recent years the focus of his work has been on sex education and this has involved primary, early years and pre-school children. He has written several articles and contributed to other publications. Most recently he has written a drug education resource pack for primary teachers.

DEBRA COSTLEY is currently undertaking research in the area of special needs education at the University of Warwick. Prior to this she taught in a variety of special school and mainstream settings. Whilst working in a school for pupils with 'moderate learning difficulties' she devised a project to deliver the National Curriculum through the cross-curricular themes. She was seconded for two terms to develop this approach with colleagues from other schools. She is committed to highlighting the importance of the cross-curricular themes, skills and dimensions within the whole curriculum context.

DEBBIE EPSTEIN lectures in Women's Studies and Education in the Centre for Research and Education on Gender at London University's Institute of Education, thus bringing together her commitment to feminism and the practice of teaching. As well as working on issues of equality in education, she is also working (with Deborah Lynn Steinberg) on a feminist analysis of the *Oprah Winfrey Show*. Recent publications include: *Changing Classroom Cultures: anti-racism, politics and schools* and *Challenging Lesbian and Gay Inequalities in Education. Schooling Sexualities: Lesbian and Gay Oppression, Identities and Education* (with Richard Johnson) is forthcoming.

PETER LANG is currently a Senior Lecturer in education at Warwick University, having previously taught for 13 years in both primary and secondary schools. His particular research interests are 'pupil perspectives', the development of effective affective schools and the nature and value of circle time. He has been involved in the editing of several books including one on Personal and Social Education (PSE) in the primary school. He is co-editor of a series on PSE and pastoral care, co-founded the journal *Pastoral Care in Education* and has been its papers' editor for twelve years. He has published a number of papers on PSE and related areas and has most recently been involved in researching and writing about PSE in an international context. He works regularly with pupils in a first school near his home.

VAL MILLMAN is adviser for Careers Education and Equal Opportunities with Coventry City Council. She has taught in both primary and secondary schools and has been involved in a variety of research and curriculum development projects. She has written about these in a number of educational books and journals. She is pleased to have survived, along with many colleagues in schools, LEAs and higher education, the onslaught of recent years upon those areas of the curriculum to which she is most committed and which provide the subject of her chapter in this book. She remains firmly convinced that it is these areas that offer the foundations for life-long learning and that their time will come again, soon.

LINA PATEL came to Britain from Kenya. She studied at the Institute of Education, Birbeck College. Formerly a teacher in East London schools, she has worked as an advisory teacher in the former Inner London Education Authority (ILEA), as a coordinator for equal opportunities for seven London Boroughs while based at the University of London Institute of Education and as coordinator for multi-cultural education in Haringey. She is currently employed as Lecturer in Environmental Studies in the Department of Teaching Studies at the University of North London.

ALISTAIR ROSS is Professor of Primary Education at the University of North London, where he has taught since 1985. For ten years before this he worked as a classroom teacher in inner London primary schools. His current responsibilities include his work as Research Director for the Faculty of Humanities and Teacher Education and he runs the Primary Schools and Industry Centre, a small unit researching children's economic understanding. He is a founder member of the International Association for Children's Social and Economics Education and editor of the Association's journal.

ANNE SINCLAIR TAYLOR is a Lecturer at the Institute of Education, University of Warwick. Prior to this she taught in a variety of mainstream and special settings and has worked predominantly with pupils with complex needs and challenging behaviour. She was head of a special unit on a mainstream campus, which promoted the integration of pupils from the unit and mainstream. Her research on integration has convinced her of the importance of taking pupils' views into account when evaluating educational provision.

IRAM SIRAJ-BLATCHFORD is Senior Lecturer in Early Childhood Education at the Institute of Education, University of London. She has held posts at the University of Warwick and in primary and nursery classrooms. She has researched and published widely on early years' education, teacher education and 'race', methodology and epistemology and teacher professionalism. She is the author of several books including *The Early Years: Laying the Foundations for Racial Equality* (Trentham Books 1994) and *Praxis Makes Perfect: Critical Educational Research for Social Justice* (Education Now 1994).

JOHN SIRAJ-BLATCHFORD has taught in secondary, and more recently in junior and infant classrooms. His current role as a Senior Lecturer in Education at Westminster College in Oxford involves him in providing a range of professional and subject focused courses for students in initial teacher education. He also provides INSET courses and teaches and supervises practising teachers for the colleges part-time M.Ed. programme. He has researched and published a number of papers concerned with citizenship, anti-racism, and science and technology education.

BALBIR KAUR SOHAL is an advisory teacher for Equal Opportunities working for Coventry Education Department. She is a black woman, born in India and raised in England. Although she initially taught history she later branched out into English, English as a second language and multi-cultural studies. As a member of a curriculum support team set up in Coventry in 1986 to ensure the permeation of multi-cultural/anti-racist education in predominantly 'white' schools, Balbir has worked in all phases from nursery through to higher education. She has been involved in working with parents, governors and the 'community' as well as providing training for the social services and government health departments.

JANICE WALE is an advisory teacher for Equal Opportunities working for Coventry Education Department. She initially trained as a primary teacher but began her educational career in further and community education. Part of this work involved teaching English as a 'second language' to various groups of Asian women. This was an experience from which she maintains that she learnt far more than she actually taught. Janice then gained several years teaching experience in early years' classrooms. As a member of the Coventry Curriculum Support Team set up to ensure the permeation of multi-cultural/anti-racist education in predominantly 'white' schools, Janice has worked in all phases, with parents, governors and the 'community' as well as providing training for other agencies.

1

JOHN and IRAM SIRAJ-BLATCHFORD

Cross-curricular skills, themes and dimensions: an introduction

This book is concerned with those aspects of the primary curriculum that have been referred to as the cross-curricular elements (National Curriculum Council (NCC) 1990). Some of the contributors to this volume are highly critical of the (former) NCC in its provision of, or failure to provide, guidance. However, all of the contributors identify aspects upon which good primary practice may be developed in the interests of children, their families and communities. The contributors have in common a commitment to, and vision of, the sort of just and egalitarian future society that the democratic realization of these interests represents.

Concern has been expressed throughout the primary teaching profession regarding the terms of both the imposition and the more recent revisions of the National Curriculum. While the need to protect the breadth and balance of the primary curriculum has been recognized (Alexander 1992), it has been widely felt that the essential character of children's learning in the primary phase has been ignored by the introduction of a subject-based National Curriculum (Dadds 1992; David et al. 1992; Hammersley and Scarth 1993; Siraj-Blatchford 1993). This is the perspective of many primary classroom teachers and it is a perspective that has too often been ignored in the past (Harlen 1993; Siraj-Blatchford 1994).

As Janet Maw has argued, in the decade from 1977 Her Majesty's Inspectorate (HMI) in England and Wales developed and refined an influential discourse of the 'whole curriculum' (Maw 1993). Since the passing of the 1988 Education Reform Act this discourse has been increasingly marginalized and replaced by a subject-based National Curriculum. This book argues that children, as active learners, need the framework of a more holistic curriculum than is currently provided in the statutory National 'basic' Curriculum. It requires the full implementation of the cross-curriculum elements and should also be based upon firm understandings of *how* children learn in contemporary Britain. In this we have found the concept of a developmental curriculum (Blenkin and Kelly 1988) especially valuable, and have extended the concept further to stress the differing learning patterns which children exhibit due to the influence of social factors. We argue that these factors, including those influencing the economic, gendered and racialized experiences of children should be considered as key elements when planning the content and process of learning for individuals and for groups of children. The book thus approaches the 'delivery' of the cross-curricular issues, themes and dimensions from a perspective emphasizing the culture of primary schools and the social worlds of children.

All the contributors share a commitment to this perspective and offer their specialist experience in implementing the cross-curricular skills, themes and dimensions. Through our in-service experience and wide consultations with primary classroom teachers we have found that there is a desperate need for schools to be supported in this area of work. The primary curriculum has been overloaded with National Curriculum subject content and there is now a need, post Dearing, to re-establish breadth and balance in the primary curriculum. This book therefore aims to provide teachers and curriculum leaders with clear principles and practical examples of successful projects that have been developed to promote the cross-curriculum issues, themes and dimensions in the primary curriculum. We aim to provide whole curriculum guidance which emphasizes curriculum coherence while ensuring that the children are not marginalized in the process. We feel that this often involves integrating cross-curricular activities into the culture and ethos of the primary school and not merely the adding or bolting together of further skills, knowledge and understandings to the core and foundation subjects of the National Curriculum. The reader's attention will therefore be continually and consistently focused upon the essentially related processes of teaching and learning.

Even the youngest children bring with them into school understandings, skills, knowledge and attitudes, and it is the teacher's role to help them develop and build upon these. We recognize that learning for young children is a social activity where new skills and understandings are gained through interaction with both adults and their peers. The approaches outlined in the book are thus grounded in an essential respect and empathy for children and childhood as a distinct stage in life and not merely as a preparation for the world of adulthood. We argue, for instance, that responsibilities and decision-making are everyday experiences for children and that they need to be able to develop attitudes and skills which enable them to participate fully in their own social world.

A number of dominant yet negative influences upon children are identified throughout this book and all are reinforced by powerful media and common everyday experiences. Social class domination and deference, racism, sexism, homophobia, the intolerance of disability, economic individualism and community and environmental recklessness are all reoccurring themes. Each negatively affects the self-image of some children in schools and perhaps ultimately and even more seriously, all children's images of 'others' are affected by these influences. The children of today will be the responsible and tolerant employers, employees, landlords, tenants and citizens of tomorrow, *or they may not*. The professional responsibility lies with us as teachers, parents and adult citizens ourselves, to create or *recreate* our society in the 21st century.

The 1988 Education Reform Act (ERA)

Section 1 of the 1988 Education Reform Act places a statutory responsibility upon schools to provide 'a broad and balanced curriculum' which:

(a) promotes the spiritual, moral, cultural, mental and physical development of pupils in schools and of society; and
(b) prepares pupils for the opportunities, responsibilities and experiences of adult life.

(DES 1988: 1)

The NCC *Curriculum Guidance Three: The Whole Curriculum* (CG3) clearly states that on its own 'the National Curriculum alone will not provide the necessary breadth' (NCC 1990: 1), and that together with religious education this 'basic' curriculum should be augmented by additional subjects and key cross-curricular elements. The guidance differentiates between those elements that represent 'cross-curriculum dimensions', 'cross-curriculum skills' and 'cross-curriculum themes'.

The cross-curriculum dimensions

CG3 refers to three major dimensions that should 'permeate every aspect of the curriculum': 'gender equality', 'cultural diversity' and 'special needs of all kinds' (NCC 1990: 2). Chapters 3, 4 and 5 are specifically concerned with these dimensions. Clearly these dimensions relate to children's current experiences at school, to equality of opportunity and their access to the curriculum and also to their preparation for their present and future lives as citizens in a free and fair democratic and diverse society. These dimensions require explicit coordination to ensure that they permeate all aspects of the overt and hidden curriculum and contribute significantly to the whole school ethos.

The cross-curriculum skills

CG3 refers to six core skills that are widely used across subjects:

- communication
- numeracy
- study
- problem solving
- personal and social
- information technology.

(NCC 1990: 3)

Despite a wide acceptance of the need to develop such cross-curriculum skills, and the NCC's suggestion that 'what is beyond dispute is that in the next century these skills, together with flexibility and adaptability, will be at a premium' (NCC 1990: 3), many of these skills have been relatively neglected in the curriculum developments of the past few years. It is to be hoped that in future they will take much more of a centre stage in developments. A conference convened by primary representatives of a wide range of subject associations in 1994 called upon the School Curriculum and Assessment Authority (SCAA) to consider basing the whole framework of the primary National Curriculum around these skills. It was argued that the subject basis of the current National Curriculum orders was inappropriate for primary schools where good practice was based upon curriculum integration and topic approaches. These are powerful arguments and it is to be hoped that these proposals are seriously considered in the next review of the National Curriculum, the results of which will be implemented in the year 2000.

While subject coordinators will need, in the meantime, to audit their schemes and programmes to maximize the development of each of the academic skills referred to, and perhaps graphicacy too, we have chosen here to restrict our attention to the themes and dimensions which are more widely relevant to children's personal and social education (PSE). The development of children's communication and personal and social skills are thus especially applicable to our project.

The cross-curriculum themes

Five 'pre-eminent' themes are identified in CG3 and it is suggested that: 'It is reasonable to assume at this stage that they are *essential* [our emphasis] parts of the whole curriculum' (NCC 1990: 4). This book therefore provides in Chapters 2, 6, 7, 8 and 9 specific guidance and discussion of each of these themes. It opens with Chapter 2, concerned with the theme of citizenship education and concludes with a chapter concerned with the unifying framework provided by PSE. As the guidance document (CG3) suggests, PSE encompasses both the whole curriculum, in its 'basic' and cross-curricular elements and all of those aims, attitudes, values and procedures of the school which contribute to its overall ethos (NCC 1990). In many ways citizenship education provides the cause within which and in the interests of which, PSE must be realized. PSE thus provides the framework and citizenship the justification for our overall approach to the whole curriculum.

Whole curriculum planning

The need for in-service training of teachers in this area cannot be overstated. The overloaded National Curriculum has wreaked havoc in primary schools, and the decision to slim it down has been taken too late to avoid widespread disruption. As Iram Siraj-Blatchford argues in Chapter 4, the true 'subjects' of the curriculum are the children themselves and the whole primary curriculum must now be recentred to reflect their needs. In the absence of government support for the reintroduction of these concerns schools will need to develop their own strategies. Each of the chapters offers a basis for developing initial discussion of the issues involved. Policies may then be collaboratively formulated and these will be all the richer for involving the whole school community at various stages in their development.

The formulation of policies may be followed by an audit of the contribution of each of the dimensions, skills and themes to each of the school's existing policies and to the relevant practices. CG3 (NCC 1990: 8) suggests that teachers may be assisted in this by local education authority advisers and inspectors and that they should involve school governors and parents and may also usefully involve children: 'Involving pupils sensitively in the process of curriculum review could help to identify the extent to which the curriculum they experience matches that intended by the school'.

Given the range and number of cross-curricular elements to be addressed this will inevitably involve a very long process and schools will need to prioritize particular elements for short-term development. The results of these audits can then be compiled and cross-referenced to identify those aspects of the policies already satisfied and those requiring more attention. This is an important stage as developments will be stronger if they are based upon the best of the school's existing practices in each area. The final stage of the process will involve setting short- and long-term targets for the implementation of development. Short-term targets with agreed deadlines ensures that progress is seen to have been made and this in itself encourages further development towards the long-term ends. The process will clearly be facilitated by distributing responsibility for the review processes throughout the school. This may involve changes or additions to job specifications but, as with any other curriculum development initiative, wherever possible such changes will be most effective when linked to staff development opportunities and promotions.

References

Alexander, R. (1992) *Policy and Practice in Primary Education*. London: Routledge.

Blenkin, G. and Kelly, A. (eds) (1988) *Early Childhood Education: A Developmental Curriculum*. London: Paul Chapman.

Dadds, M. (1992) Monty Python and the three wise men. *Cambridge Journal of Education*, 22(2): 129–43.

David, T., Curtis, A. and Siraj-Blatchford, I. (1992) *Effective Teaching in the Early Years*. Stoke on Trent: Trentham Books.

Department of Education and Science (DES) (1988) *Education Reform Act 1988*. London: HMSO.

Hammersley, M. and Scarth, J. (1993) Beware of wise men bearing gifts. *British Educational Research Journal*, 19(4): 489–99.

Harlen, W. (1993) Is the child being squeezed out? *Times Educational Supplement*, 25 June.

Maw, J. (1993) The National Curriculum Council and the Whole Curriculum: reconstruction of a discourse? *Curriculum Studies*, 1(1): 55–74.

National Curriculum Council (NCC) (1990) *Curriculum Guidance Three: The Whole Curriculum*. York: NCC.

Siraj-Blatchford, I. (1994) Back to the future? *Times Educational Supplement*, 24 June.

Siraj-Blatchford, J. (1993) Objectional objectivity. *Early Years – Journal of TAC-TYC*, 13(2) Spring: 50–3.

2

JOHN SIRAJ-BLATCHFORD

Little citizens: helping children to help each other

Editors' introduction

As we have already discussed in Chapter 1, this book is fundamentally concerned with the development of democratic behaviour through children's experience of the school in, and as part of, their community. Citizenship is thus taken as the theme of this chapter. The following pages provide a critical evaluation of the guidance and resources available to primary schools in this area. It is argued that the democratisation of childhood itself represents a major challenge for educationalists. This is illustrated by the use of case studies of children's work in a primary school council. It is suggested that the framework provided in *Curriculum Guidance Eight: Education for Citizenship* (CG8) (NCC 1990) offers a valuable basis for developing the active collaboration of children in their primary education but that this can be developed further to include work across the whole primary curriculum and in pursuit of a holistic education for all.

Introduction

CG8 emphasizes that education for citizenship should be concerned with responsibilities and rights in the child's *present* as well as in preparation for their adult life. The document suggests that schools should lay the foundations for positive, participative citizenship in two ways:

(i) by helping pupils to acquire and understand essential information;
(ii) by providing them with opportunities and incentives to participate in all aspects of school life.

(NCC 1990: 1)

While pupils need to be informed of their present and future rights and responsibilities as laid down in the various national and international charters, conventions and legislation (see United Nations 1989; Runnymede Trust 1993), this chapter is primarily concerned with the latter aspect which provides a much more fundamental challenge to the manner in which learning in many schools is currently organized. While both elements will contribute to encouraging children's active and informed participation as adults in democratic government, their involvement in democratic schooling provides unique opportunities to practise and develop the skills, values and attitudes essential to their *effective* participation.

Schooling for democracy

Harding (1990) provides an account of an interaction between a Chinese student and a Western television journalist in Tiananmen Square in 1989. The student claimed that what Chinese students and intellectuals wanted from the West was its 'advanced technology'. The journalist asked if that was all, were they not interested in democracy? She answered: 'Yes, but only if they are *advanced ideas* [my emphasis] about democracy'. In much of the recent educational writing on the subject we seem somehow to have lost any such *qualitative* conception of democracy. But democracy is not simply a term that describes *our* particular (peculiar?) form of government; it is not simply a description of a static and complete set of political principles and practices that have been achieved, it is also an ideal that is to be worked towards. It is a form of government that has developed as the electoral franchise has been extended, and as equality of opportunity and 'race' discrimination legislation is implemented. It is an ideal that may ultimately only be fully realized when power is decentralized and communication technologies are developed to enable government by the people rather than by their elected representatives.

Democratic 'rights' provision is developing to safeguard the interests of individuals and minorities and a number of future participatory democratic models are conceivable. With the extension of such rights the image of mob rule should no longer be plausible. A whole range of possibilities for community self-government are included in Benello and Roussopoulos (1971). Power might be radically decentralized to create small local community units that would have a veto over national decisions. Alternatively we might move towards alternative methods of decision making. Cook and Morgan (1971), argue that principles of co-determination, including the involvement of workers participating in industry and students in education, would ensure that specialized information would be available to decision makers. Dahl (1985: 94) suggested that worker control of their industries would not only reduce feelings of alienation, but also 'improve the quality of democracy in the government of the state by transforming us into better citizens'.

The task of ministers may yet become to 'faithfully execute' the popular will, rather than to have power delegated to them by a minority of the population, as is currently the case in modern Western 'democracies'. Our government is currently selected according to the wishes of the largest minority of those who choose to vote. Ultimately we could aspire to move beyond the current state of political stagnation, where many ordinary people fail to participate and are disillusioned by the inertia of the established political parties that fail to represent their views or interests. The major parties are supported by expensive media campaigns and restrictive electoral laws and are thus unchallenged and perhaps currently unchallengeable. The failure of increasing numbers of citizens to register or vote in elections is evidence in itself of the failure of the system of representative democracy as a whole. So what is to be done and what role does the school have in the further development of participatory democracy?

Schools play a major role in reproducing the form of our society, providing an important means of socialization. As Section One of the Education Reform Act (1988: 1) puts it, the curriculum is designed to 'promote the spiritual, moral, cultural, mental and physical development' of 'society' as well as of pupils. It should also: 'Prepare such pupils for the opportunities, responsibilities and experiences of adult life'. It is in these contexts that the theme of citizenship can be seen as crucial.

All curricula necessarily represent a selection of content and of pedagogic approach. We decide what we are to teach according to our decisions regarding what is to be achieved in doing so. Social aims are translated into curriculum aims and then applied, and as Dewey (1971) suggested none of this has any meaning at all unless we define the kind of future society that we have in mind. As a society committed to participatory democracy, our aim must be to educate our children to be participating democrats.

An increasing body of writing in recent years, particularly in those areas of scholarship that have been concerned with gender, sexuality and 'race' equality, has drawn greater attention to the pluralist nature of our society. In the fields of educational sociology and in cultural studies, this recognition of social heterogeneity, largely fuelled by postmodern and post-structuralist influences, has led many to acknowledge the limitations of a liberal democratic politics based upon largely assumed and stereotyped group interests. As Parker (1994) has put it, in this sense:

> Pluralism itself needs to be reformulated in order to avoid the essentializing tendencies of much liberal and radical thinking about diversity that considers men to be such and such because they are men, and Japanese to be so and so because they are Japanese. In the same way, women are this way; blacks are that way; Hispanics are . . .; lesbians are . . .; the working class is . . . and so on down a stereotype-littered civic back alley from which no one, and no group, escapes.
>
> (Parker 1994: 18)

The challenge is, as Parker goes on to argue, to recognize individual and group identities without 'etching them in primordial stone' (ibid.). To create, in Dewey's terms a 'larger public' that embraces the 'little publics'. This will be a public that is not bonded by a common culture, but one that celebrates diversity in 'a broad political comradeship' (Parker 1994: 18). Parker argues that in practice this will involve educators most significantly in the elevation of civic discourse, particularly, although not exclusively, in promoting face-to-face discussion of public problems. Also:

> Discussion itself should be studied, and discussion competence developed. Who associates in discussion? Is difference repressed, tolerated, or respected? How do particular discussion forums advantage some groups and disadvantage others? How is participants' cultural self-knowledge (i.e. cultural capital) addressed? How can consensus be reached and obstacles overcome? What about persons who disagree with a consensus? Discussion, then, is prominent in the curriculum, not only as an instructional method, but as subject matter and as a form of democratic action.
>
> (Parker 1994: 23)

Children need to be exposed to conflicting perspectives including public controversies and perspectives that have been developed by groups in their resistance and struggle against oppression. As Don Rowe (1992) has observed it is ironic that in recent years it has been the political Right, the very group which has called most loudly for the teaching of moral standards and respect for the law, that has inhibited much of the development of these approaches. Another inhibiting factor has been apparent within the education establishment. Crude applications of Piagetian child development theories have served to limit the development of curriculum and thus of children. 'Cognitive developmental stages' have been applied to children and the curriculum matched to the 'levels' that research showed they already achieve rather than being set to surpass them.

Similarly the work of psychological research concerned with moral development has led classroom teachers and some other educationalists to put aside aspects of holistic education in favour of less demanding approaches (see Solomon 1993). In all of these cases, while the research has identified what children can do and understand, without educational support, the findings have been uncritically applied to suggest essential limits to children's innate capabilities. These perspectives are reminiscent of the pathological, child deficit approaches applied to girls' underachievement in the physical sciences and to black and ethnic minority children a decade ago.

Many areas of the curriculum have thus been neglected in primary schools and work postponed for later (less influential) years. Thankfully, alternative understandings of children's learning are gaining ground throughout the profession and these alternative perspectives are quickly acquiring a strong empirical base. They are founded on the work of Lev Vygotsky, Jerome Bruner (1960) and Margaret Donaldson (1978), who emphasized the importance of educating the whole child, of revisiting themes through a spiral curriculum and of supporting children's achievement. Vygotsky, in particular, provides a model to explain how the teacher, the child's peers or other adults may 'scaffold' their achievement within a zone of proximal development (Vygotsky 1962). Children learn their 'personal' political attitudes in the micro-politics of everyday life (Harber 1980; Harwood 1985). As Ross (1987) has argued children are aware of and are members of society from birth.

Children should learn democratic values, they should learn to appreciate that *all* their demands *cannot* be satisfied if minority interests are to be respected. They should learn how to listen as well as how to talk, and how to take turns. They should learn to check their facts, to suspend their judgment and as Parker (1994: 27, citing Mathews 1994) argues to allow 'positions to develop *through* discussion rather than only defending positions held before'. They should also be encouraged to enter into a variety of small and large associations with others, and to recognize the essential limitations of the current forms of party politics.

In many ways the emphasis of the Report of the Commission on Citizenship, *Encouraging Citizenship* (1990) is consistent with such an approach. The commission, patronized by Bernard Weatherill, then Speaker of the House of Commons, chose not to confine itself to the formal and existing civil and political structures but to ground its recommended provision upon international charters and conventions on human rights and upon voluntary associations. As the summary states:

> The challenge to our society in the late twentieth century is to create conditions where all who wish can become actively involved, can understand and participate, can influence, persuade, campaign and whistleblow, and in the making of decisions can work together for the mutual good.
>
> (Commission on Citizenship 1990: xv)

Children as citizens

The school offers, as a community in itself, a valuable (perhaps ideal) site for democratic endeavour. The association of diverse groups of children and adults, students and teachers, parents and governors, boys and girls, rich and poor, black and white, abled and disabled as well as various religious affiliations, the police and the press, all with various powers and status, offers a potent educational theatre.

CG8 suggests that young citizens should develop a knowledge and understanding of:

- the nature of community;
- roles and relationships in a pluralist society;
- the duties, responsibilities and rights of being a citizen.

In addition, five contexts are specified within which citizenship may be explored. In an inservice training (INSET) manual for secondary schools, Tilley (1991) provides a matrix shown here in Table 2.1 which details the eight components included in the guidance and relates them to the other cross-curriculum themes.

Table 2.1   Citizenship matrix

	EIU	Health	Careers	Environmental education
Broad themes				
Nature of community	√	√	√	
Pluralism in society	√	√	√	√
Duties, rights and responsibilities	√	√	√	√
Everyday contexts				
The family		√		
Democracy in action	√	√	√	√
The law	√	√	√	√
Work, employment and leisure	√	√	√	
Public services	√	√	√	√

Source: Tilley (1991)

Chapter 8 of this book suggests that in many ways the relationships between groups and communities and the nature of local work, employment and leisure activities *do* influence the environment. In Chapters 6, 7 and 8 we also show how the family is directly implicated in the development of the child's awareness of economic and industrial understanding (EIU), of careers and of the environment. The citizenship matrix can in fact be shown to include *all* of the themes and, of course, all of the cross-curriculum dimensions as well. In Chapter 9, Bennett, Sohal and Wale also discuss a number of the issues and controversies surrounding the family. The subject of democracy and the need to teach children about their legal rights and responsibilities has been discussed in this chapter. In Chapters 6 and 7, Alistair Ross and Val Millman explore a range of relevant issues concerned with work and employment. The remaining subjects of 'leisure' and of 'public services' can be seen as especially relevant to the development of active and participatory citizenship in the context of the school community. This is a subject to which I shall now turn.

Democratic schooling

I remember once seeing a cartoon in the educational press that showed a teacher with a small child. As I remember it, both figures were highly stereotyped, the teacher wearing a gown and mortar board, the child, a boy in school uniform, dishevelled with tie askew. The child is asking the teacher: 'If education is so important then why aren't we learning about it in school?' I have always thought that the child had a valid point. Young children, perhaps inevitably, see a major distinction between school 'work' and play. Despite the efforts of early childhood educators, many parents and teachers still make this distinction. If we are ever to convince others of the developmental value of play perhaps we should begin with our own pupils and start to convince them that what they learn at their leisure is often as important and meaningful as that provided in their 'lessons'. The school is a major public service institution and an understanding and active involvement in the 'delivery' of this service would provide a very meaningful basis for developing children's understanding of other services, both local and national.

Children have all kinds of rights, responsibilities and duties within all school contexts. These relate to behaviours within and outside the classroom, and involve their interactions with all of those who make up the internal and local community: their peers, the local community itself, parents, ancillary workers, school visitors and teachers. In the primary years citizenship should first be centred upon the child's own experience and these local contexts are therefore fundamental. Citizenship education is transferable and strongly influenced by the immediate community (Torney 1971). Having begun to develop the relevant attitudes, skills, knowledge and understanding within this limited although demanding context, children will be in a stronger position to apply them to the wider national and global contexts that will support their further understanding of international interdependence.

The Plan-Do-Review cycle has enjoyed considerable success in a variety of pre-school and infant settings and has shown that even the youngest children can usefully be given responsibility to plan their own work. As CG8 suggests: 'The aim is to develop the ability to exercise choice responsibility' (NCC 1990: 11). Groupwork provides opportunities for developing cooperation and decision making. Lynch (1991) suggests several useful 'effective schools' criteria, based on the concept of global citizenship education:

- a democratic classroom ethos, giving rise to feelings of trust among pupils and between teachers and pupils;
- collaborative and cooperative approaches to help the development of organic social relationships and foster mutuality and moral reciprocity;
- active participation, including simulation, role-playing and varied group composition, as well as social engagement;
- emphasis on character development, which will include skills of conflict resolution;
- rational, holistic approaches to knowledge and learning, using methods which appeal to the judgement of the learners;
- help for pupils in evolving and clarifying their own value systems, using situations involving value dilemmas;
- emphasis on open rather than closed tasks and questions;
- multiple approaches, including different media, strategies and locations;
- inclusion of pedagogies involving social responsibility and actioning;
- high intellectual expectations in both cognitive and affective domains;
- explicit commitment to global human rights as the basis for all interaction in the classroom;
- linked, supportive assessment methods, orientated to student success.

(Lynch 1991: 23)

School newsletters may provide a powerful forum for involving children in decision making concerned with the school organization and environment. This could be extended to involve the children in local campaigns. The Frinet educational model, developed in France, was centred around such campaigns and the school printing press. Another very powerful forum for developing participation may be provided by a school council.

A primary school council

Research conducted for the Commission on Citizenship by Ken Fogelman shows that as many as 60 per cent of the secondary schools surveyed had 'school council or year or house councils, on which pupils are represented' (Commission on Citizenship 1990: 86). School councils are relatively rare in primary schools, yet they have been shown to be highly successful. One Coventry primary school elected representatives from each classroom, from reception to year six. The elections themselves provided a valuable context for citizenship education. There being no prescribed method of election, the children had to decide upon their own arrangement each year. As one of the year six pupils, Daniel, explained:

> First of all we started off with how we would vote, whether it would be a person from each register group in the area, a boy and a girl, or one from each year. We voted for one from each area and then we nominated a couple of people, about six from each area and then we wrote them down on slips of paper and the teachers put them in a box and Elizabeth got nineteen and I got fifteen. But it was funny how it turned out because we got a boy and a girl and sixth years from each register group.
>
> (Siraj-Blatchford 1992: 37)

Most of the classes chose to adopt some form of secret ballot, some chose proportional representation, while with others it was 'first past the post'. The representatives met twice a term and discussed a wide range of issues which included playtime activities, codes of behaviour, litter problems, the school uniform and charity events. The council elected a chairperson at the beginning of each meeting and each class discussed the issues posted on the agenda before each meeting, so that the representatives were briefed on their groups' feelings on the issues. Suggestion boxes were also employed to obtain as wide a range of concerns and perspectives to discuss as possible. Right from the beginning the children were quite sure that the council was beneficial to the school as a whole. Marie, year two, commented: 'I think it's a good idea for when you're grown up and you're voting for something' (ibid.: 37), and Debbie, year four, felt that: 'It's useful because you think of ideas that might be better for the school which might do more good' (ibid.: 37). Perhaps the best reason for having such a council, and for citizenship education in general, was actually voiced by one of the school's youngest councillors, Helen from year one: 'I think you should have the school council because it would make less wars and when people grow up they could make more votes' (ibid.: 37).

You, me and us!

A good deal of evidence is now available that suggests that even very young children have the enthusiasm and ability to formulate and evaluate arguments and think critically in contexts within which they are actively involved (Siraj-Blatchford 1992; Costello 1993). In 1994 a major new initiative in the form of a resource pack was launched, sponsored by the Home Office and entitled *You, Me, Us!* (Rowe and Newton 1994). It provides a range of citizenship materials specifically written for primary school children. The pack adopts a 'social responsibility approach' which is based upon a conflict model of citizenship emphasizing justice and rights. Stories are used to raise moral questions and conflicts for the children to discuss. One example provides a dramatic account of a classroom incident that relates to key stage two experiences. A girl called Sally gets into trouble for splashing paint on the floor when it was not really her fault. She then agrees to a friend helping her complete a peg bag in time for her mother's birthday the next day and spends her lunch time cleaning up the mess. Her friend is not really allowed to be in the classroom at all and Sally allows her teacher to believe that she had completed the peg bag herself. The story provides a context to discuss 'telling tales' and the question of whether or not it is ever acceptable to break a rule for a 'good' reason. Other stories cover aspects of law, friendship issues, the fair treatment of property, power and authority, respect for others and environmental and community issues. All have been trialled in schools and have shown their value in developing critical reflection on justice, rights and responsibilities. As Rowe (1992) observes:

> The whole approach encourages pupils to challenge ideas and, in so doing, they reflect on experiences and values drawn from the different communities to which they belong, including the home, family, friendship groups, faith groups, school and the wider community.
>
> (Rowe 1992: 183)

This will undoubtably be the major value of these materials, to stimulate discussions of real events and to work out conflicts and problems in open cooperation within the classroom community.

Conclusion: making a start

Teachers may usefully begin by carrying out an audit of the opportunities offered to children to exercise responsibility within their own classrooms, and with their own pupils, throughout the school. This may serve to raise awareness but ultimately the widest involvement of children, staff and parents is desirable. Tilley (1991) provides a 'curriculum planning card set' which, although developed for secondary schools might usefully be applied to match the various skills, values, attitudes and understandings that are covered by specific experiences.

The framework of CG8 offers a valuable basis for developing the active collaboration of children in their primary education. Education for democracy and the democratization of childhood may represent a major challenge for educationalists but ultimately our future may depend upon it.

References

Bennello, C. and Roussopoulos, D. (1971) *The Case for Participatory Democracy*. New York: Grossman.

Bruner, J. (1960) *The Process of Education*. New York: Vintage Books.

Commission on Citizenship (1990) *Encouraging Citizenship*. London: HMSO.

Cook, T. and Morgan, P. (1971) *Participatory Democracy*. New York: Harper and Row.

Costello, P. (1993) *Education, Citizenship and Critical Thinking*. Wrexham: North East Wales Institute.

Dahl, R. (1985) *A Preface to Economic Democracy*. Berkeley: University of California Press.

Department of Education and Science (DES) (1988) *Education Reform Act 1988*. London: HMSO.

Dewey, J. (1971) *Experience and Education*. London: Collier-Macmillan.

Donaldson, M. (1978) *Children's Minds*. London: Fontana.

Harber, C. (1980) Teaching the politics of everyday life. *Social Science Teacher*, (10)2: (pull out).

Harding, V. (1990) *Hope and History: Why We Must Share the Story of the Movement*. New York: Orbis.

Harwood, D. (1985) We need political, not Political education for 5–13 year olds. *Education*, 3(13): 12–18.

Lynch, J. (1991) *Education for Citizenship in a Multicultural Society*. New York: Cassell.

Mathews, D. (1994) *Politics for the People*. Urbana: University of Illinois Press.

National Curriculum Council (NCC) (1990) *Curriculum Guidance Eight: Citizenship Education*. York: NCC.

Parker, W. (1994) *Curriculum for Democracy: Aims and Principles*. Paper presented at the annual meeting of the American Educational Research Association, New Orleans, April.

Ross, A. (1987) Political education in the primary school, in C. Harber (ed.) *Political Education in Britain*. Lewes: Falmer Press.

Rowe, D. (1992) The citizen as a moral agent: the development of a continuous and progressive conflict-based citizenship curriculum. *Curriculum* 13(3): 178–88.

Rowe, D. and Newton, J. (1994) *You, Me, Us!* London: The Citizenship Foundation.

Runnymede Trust (1993) *Equality Assurance in Schools*. Stoke on Trent: Trentham Books.

Siraj-Blatchford, J. (1992) School citizens. *Child Education*, May: 37.

Solomon, J. (1993) *Teaching Science, Technology and Society*. Buckingham: Open University Press.

Tilley, G. (ed.) (1991) *Cross-Curricular Issues: An INSET Manual for Secondary Schools*. Harlow: Longman.

Torney, J. (1971) Socialisation of attitudes towards the legal system. *Journal of Social Issues*, 27(2).

United Nations (UN) (1989) *Teaching Human Rights: Practical Activities for Primary and Secondary Schools*. New York: UN.

Vygotsky, L. (1962) *Thought and Language*. Cambridge, Mass.: MIT Press.

3

ANNE SINCLAIR TAYLOR
and DEBRA COSTLEY

Effective schooling for all:
the 'special educational needs'
dimension

Editors' introduction

In this important contribution Anne Sinclair Taylor and Debra
Costley suggest that the individual needs of children should be
paramount in defining educational provision. They argue that
while, in the past, children have often been the last to be
consulted, recent legislation provides at least the potential for
developing a truly child centred focus. Anne and Debra thus
provide what may be considered the limit case for involving
children in the determination of their educational provision.
They argue that while many of those children with the greatest
'special needs' may be less able to articulate their needs and
point of view, every effort should be made to encourage them.
Practical strategies are provided to encourage all children to
contribute to the process of providing effective education.

The chapter provides an authoritative account of the
historical development of 'special needs'. The pathological
nature of popular definitions are discussed and it is argued that
an education seeking to provide for the individual needs of all
children would be a truly inclusive system. Children's 'special
needs' are currently defined according to the cognitive,
communicative, physical or sensory deficits they exhibit when
compared to their peer group. The educational problematic is
thus defined in terms of the child's 'problem' in meeting the
'normal' demands of schooling. An alternative perspective

would consider the problems and special needs of the school in providing an entitlement for all. Anne and Debra adopt such a perspective to question in-class and externally divisive setting and streaming practices and give priority to children's rights.

Whose need is it anyway?

Most children with 'special needs' are in mainstream schools. The Office of Population Censuses and Surveys (1989) identified 360,000 children under the age of 16 with 'impairments'. Just under two-thirds of these children are educated in ordinary schools. Only 62,000 of these pupils had statements which defined their 'special educational needs' and the means of meeting those needs. Many children with 'special needs' therefore are in mainstream schools and are members of ordinary classes. Throughout their careers, primary teachers will inevitably encounter children with a wide range of learning and behavioural needs.

This chapter discusses strategies for responding to the needs of a wide range of pupils. It addresses issues which relate to the preparation of pupils for the ultimate purpose of schooling, 'adult citizenship'. We refer to the term 'adult citizenship' as we feel it a mark of how we view childhood and adolescence that adulthood and citizenship are implicitly conflated. While it is clearly necessary to reconcile ageism with a sensitivity to the needs and capacities of individuals by maturity, are children still not citizens? Or are children merely seen as 'incomplete adults hanging around and waiting to grow up'? (Rosen 1994).

Prior to the 1989 Children Act (Department of Health 1989) the legal and structural framework which governed children's educational and social experiences was authoritarian, reflecting the view that children are the property of their parents, or during the school day their teachers. The children who are most vulnerable in this respect are those with 'special needs', whose relationship with the system has tended towards powerlessness and subordination. This may be one reason why much research on the effectiveness of provision has failed to take children's views into account. The consumers of the education system have been perceived to be parents. This has been communicated through various channels, in particular, The Parents Charter and its updated and aligned documents (Department of Education and Science (DES) 1991; Department for Education (DFE) 1994b). It is the view of the writers that the real 'consumers' of education are children. Only the children themselves can speak about their experiences and perceptions of the social and pedagogic aspects of schooling. Planning educational provision responsively and effectively requires that we tap into pupils' views. In this chapter we will consider how we can enfranchise children (particularly those with so-called 'special needs') into the legal and educational system which governs their lives. Before looking at the curricular implications of an inclusive approach to the schooling of pupils with 'special needs' some discussion about the concept of 'special educational needs' (SEN) will take place.

The concept of 'special educational need'

The term 'special needs' became generally applied in educational circles after the 1981 Education Act (DES 1981) (now readopted under the 1993 Education Act DES 1993), as a result of its popularization by Baroness Warnock and her committee. It marked a shift in the discourse of special education by its avoidance of any reference to disability. However, while the generic term 'special educational needs' replaced disability or handicap, its interpretation under the 1981 (now 1993) Act meant that it still covered the old range of disabilities or deficits. The 1981 Act has at its heart an entrenched, medically based, deficit model of disability. While labels such as the term 'maladjusted', originally used in the 1994 Educational Act, were changed to emotional and behavioural difficulties and 'educationally subnormal' to moderate learning difficulties, the basic discourse of deficit informed practice. Labels were amended, laundered and updated but they served the same purpose, to allocate groups of children, by their deficits, to differential education (Fulcher 1989).

The 1993 Act and *Code of Practice on the Identification and Assessment of Special Needs* (DFE 1994a), by readopting a taxonomy of deficits, has proved to be a great disappointment to those who have criticized the Warnock Report (DES 1978) and the 1981 Act for more than a decade. As Tony Booth says the 1993 Act and Code of Practice represent 'a lost opportunity to reconceptualise special education' (Booth 1994: 21).

'Special needs' is an umbrella term which covers a wide range of negative and ultimately discriminatory labels. Rather than descriptions focusing on similarities and common needs, the term 'special need' conveys differences and separate needs. Telling someone that a child has 'special needs' according to Tony Booth 'is almost wholly destructive . . . here is a person who is not a normal student' (ibid.).

Having artificial, legally defined boundaries between the 'normal' and 'not normal' may lead to discriminatory thinking and practice. This deficit model of assessing individual needs ultimately compromises the goals of inclusive education. Rather than thinking of 'special needs', would it therefore not be more enabling to think of individual needs; recognizing that from time to time every one of us has needs which require extra support, no matter what our physical or intellectual capacities? When needs arise, the degree to which they become manageable relates to the support given. The concept of 'special needs' is inextricably linked to the support structures available. How far then is participation for all linked to the allocation and location of resources, the teaching and learning styles employed and the curriculum content focused upon? In considering the wider issues related to this topic we will introduce a case study child, Tom.

Tom

Tom is 10; he finds school a struggle. He works more slowly than his peer group and finds concentrating on any task for more than a few minutes difficult. He is producing work more typical of a year two child, or as his teacher jokingly puts it, 'Tom is working towards work'. Tom is viewed by teachers and children alike as a problem, a bit of an outsider and this profoundly affects his self-esteem. How can this situation be improved? Currently neither Tom, his classmates nor his teachers feel any sense of harmony or purpose in terms of their working relationships. One reaction might be to argue that Tom should leave the mainstream and transfer to a special unit or school. He does not fit in and it would be better for all concerned to accept this. This solution clearly places the burden of responsibility with Tom. He is perceived as 'the problem'. Tom has been characterized by his differences (his deficits) in relation to his peer group. Thus a deficit model of viewing Tom has been operationalized, which may result in his needs being described as 'special'.

Deficit or ecology?

Deficit theories of learning and behaviour place the responsibility for any 'problem' with the child. It is the child's deficits in particular areas (for example, attention, language or overall cognitive skills) which are the source of the 'problem'. The remedy for the 'problem', therefore, is to increase the child's skills in areas of deficit so that he or she can join in everyday learning again, and become normal not special. Such an approach is both narrow and flawed, in that it decontextualizes the child's learning capacities and achievements; it fails to take into account the influences of the curriculum and the teacher. It also fails to respect or celebrate difference.

An alternative, broader approach asserts that single factor explanations for any problem are seldom satisfactory, and that Tom's problems are part of a much wider picture. This picture includes the wider influences of national and local authority policy as well as school organization and ethos. This approach argues that there is a symbiotic relationship between the school and how it facilitates and evaluates learning and the individual child's aptitudes. How far Tom's needs are viewed as special is tightly linked, therefore, to school organization (Ainscow and Tweddle 1988). While the first of these views can be described as the deficit model of 'special needs' the alternative provides an 'ecological' model. This model asserts the importance of placing a situation or set of circumstances within a wider framework for analysis. Curricular expectations, teaching style or class-room organization may be exacerbating the situation. Conversely modifica-tion in these areas may ameliorate or alter perspectives about what is happening (Thomas and Feiler 1988).

By applying the first model, the deficit approach, to solve Tom's pro-blems, a chain of events would take place, working through the Code of Practice (DFE 1994a) procedures, possibly culminating in statementing and even special school placement; while reflection about school practice would take place, it would have Tom's problems as the focus. By applying the second model, the ecological, a different chain of events takes place, one where the school scrutinizes procedures and policies, analyses teaching styles and curriculum delivery and appraises classroom organization with the intention of making changes or adaptations to practices in general.

But why would any school wish to incur the extra work this would entail merely to retain one 'problematic' pupil? (A pupil who incidentally would not show up favourably in published league tables of Standard Assessment Tasks (SATs)). Both approaches share an agenda which requires critical reflection, however they differ in their emphases. The ecological approach takes the wider view; that is, if Tom is experiencing difficulties, perhaps others are too, and the system needs therefore to respond and to change.

Effective schools

Schools are under pressure. Research conducted with 100 teachers over four years, since 1989, suggests that staff felt there had been a deterioration in their skills in catering for children with learning difficulties and that the curriculum was becoming increasingly unmanageable (Campbell and Neill 1994).

Schools are, however, required under the Education Act (1993) and the *Code of Practice on the Identification and Assessment of Special Educa-tional Needs* (DFE 1994a) to have clear strategies in place to support and cater for pupils with complex needs. Ultimately, according to the Code, it is hoped that more pupils will remain in mainstream, rather than require statementing and/or special school placements. At the same time, schools are competing in a market place for pupils. One of the criteria which schools are being judged by are successes in examination league tables. On the face of it, providing for a wide range of pupils, as well as succeeding in league tables of examination results must create a strain on the system. Tensions are apparently created by these countervailing pressures, but it is possible to reconcile them. In fact 'good practice' for all pupils, it can be argued, does reconcile both issues. Mortimore *et al.* (1988), Rutter *et al.* (1979), and the Office for Standards in Education (OFSTED) (1993), found that good practice in relation to vulnerable pupils also impacts positively on other pupils.

According to this research effective schools stress positive interactions between staff and pupils and establish an ethos which recognizes, rewards and values individuals of all ability levels within the community of the school. Brighouse and Tomlinson (1991) reinforce these findings but importantly, in relation to encouraging participation of the widest range of pupils, include the following factors:

- schools which are effective have teachers who demonstrate concern for pupils' development as individuals in society;
- show a commitment by staff to pupils' personal and social development (this includes offering effective guidance).

Healthy and effective schools, according to the research, develop a culture where aims, practice and outcomes in relation to pupils' learning and well-being are constantly questioned.

This research shows that ultimately we can judge schools by how children are encouraged to become 'capable' no matter what their individual skills and gifts (Brighouse and Tomlinson 1991). Analysis of policies and practice with regard to a child like Tom, with complex difficulties, can be highly revealing of structural and pedagogic deficiencies. Such analyses may assist development of a more effective learning environment for all pupils.

According to Brighouse and Tomlinson (1991) 'Good schooling is about developing individuality within a fraternity . . . a moral sense of themselves and their rights and duties towards other'. Teacher actions towards pupils are only one dimension of relationships within the school. Developing a climate of respect between pupils, teachers, ancillary staff and parents is also important. The quality of these relationships will be observable in interactions between children, children and teachers, teachers with each other and with parents.

School organization and integration

While all interactions reveal something of the moral climate of the school, the quality of contacts between pupils who find learning easy and those who find it more difficult can be particularly illuminating. A key determinant of the success or otherwise of the social and pedagogic integration of a wide variety of pupils is linked to the way in which schools are organized. Hargreaves (1967), Lacey (1970) and Corrigan (1979) have shown how anti-school subcultures and marginalization develop amongst pupils in the lower streams of stratified schools. This is due to pedagogic organization, based on the belief systems which prevailed in the school, rather than 'within' child characteristics. Hargreaves showed that after the first two years of secondary school, when pupils were allocated 'exam' or 'non-exam' status, pupils in the latter group, adopted a defensive alternative system of values to protect themselves from being labelled as 'failures'. Other writers have emphasized how this kind of curricular stratification leads to marginalization and lowering of self-esteem, such that a polarization of social and anti-social behaviour between higher and lower stream pupils takes place (Burgess 1983; Kyriacou 1986).

Research undertaken by Anne Sinclair Taylor, in a unit attached to a mainstream school revealed that rather than the unit promoting integration, as intended, it fostered the marginalization of its pupils. Unit pupils thought mainstream children saw them in a negative light; being a member of the unit carried with it a diminished status which resulted in social stratification. This was illustrated by how unit children thought mainstream pupils described them. A girl in the unit described how 'they [mainstream] call us unit kids and provoke us and say we are spastics. He looks like one himself', jabbing her fingers toward a mainstream boy, while two boys said how 'Mainstream kids tease you, they see the unit as a place for mental people less better than themselves'; and 'other kids say the unit is for dunce people and spastics who ain't got much sense'.

Unit pupils' views were compared to those of children in mainstream, teachers in both unit and main school and to observations made by the researcher. Views collated from varying sources reinforced what children from the unit said. Of all the sources of data, however, the pupils' views were the most illuminating (Sinclair Taylor, 1995).

While the research referred to was undertaken in secondary schools, it has relevance for primary education where there is a discernible move towards consideration of grouping or streaming for teaching (Alexander *et al.* 1992). This will have major implications for pupils whose needs are described as 'special'.

Policy and planning for SEN pupils

How might schools consider their position with regard to pupils with SEN? How might they decide to organize learning for all pupils? According to Cullen (1994: 28): 'The essential activity of a successful school is persistent questioning. This is the engine of vitality and self-renewal'.

Schools evolving and updating their policies with regard to pupils with SEN might usefully begin the process of evaluation by encouraging staff to confront their beliefs about children's needs and rights and the teacher's role with regard to them. It is important for an underpinning philosophy to be agreed before a working policy is developed and procedures implemented (Palmer *et al.* 1994). Any whole school policy or mission statement has to take account of the beliefs of all of those involved. If there is little genuine support for a particular approach from governors, teachers, parents and pupils, policy and practice will flounder (Warnock 1994). The literature contains many examples where there has been a divergence between policy and practice in LEAs and schools (see McNay and Ozga 1985; Troyna 1993).

For teachers to feel genuine ownership of, and commitment to, a 'special needs' policy it must be applicable and appropriate to that school context. So if, for example, one of the belief statements which underpins such a policy is 'responsibility for teaching pupils with special needs lies with their class teacher', then this will only work if all of those concerned agree. The extent of agreement may be due to deeply held convictions, but with the demands of the National Curriculum in often large and growing classes, many will feel that this can only be done with adequate resources, support and additional expertise (Campbell and Neill 1994).

Inclusive policy developments are predicated on conceptions of human rights, on the rights of the 'disabled' to access aspects of life enjoyed by other citizens. Paul Boateng quoted in Edwards and Fogelman (1993: 7) emphasizes three elements necessary for citizenship: 'a sense of belonging; the capacity to gain access; the ability to participate'. People with 'special needs' have been subjected to marginalization from 'normal' living; for example being bussed out of their neighbourhoods to special schools and units. Those with 'special needs' have been denied access not only to public buildings and facilities but to employment, an adequate income and housing (Tisdall 1994: 5). Participation has been compromised on many levels from the purely physical through to the social and emotional. People with 'special needs' have been characterized by their passivity and dependency and their lack of rights or opportunities to exercise responsibility (Tomlinson 1982).

Recently, however, the Disability Rights Movement has begun to shift the rights of those with 'special needs' up the political agenda. It is through the endeavours of those with disabilities themselves that there has been a push towards anti-discrimination legislation in this country. When the Disabled Rights Bill floundered in 1994, ostensibly due to financial constraints, there was a well publicized outcry. Some people with disabilities chained themselves to buses outside Parliament, to underline their strength of feeling. Educational policy makers would do well to take heed of these developments. It would be naïve to think that the push for anti-discrimination legislation will not surface again, or that it will not influence educational provision of the future (Mason and Rieser 1994).

The importance of cross-curricular skills

Schools have the opportunity to be proactive in this area by helping young people to develop personal and social skills which will encourage self-confidence and advocacy. The cross-curricular skills of communication, numeracy, study skills, problem-solving skills, personal and social skills and information technology handling skills can be placed at the centre of learning for all pupils. These skills offer pupils the basic tools for coping with other aspects of schooling and life in general. Their importance is also reflected clearly in the Dearing Report's advice for primary school teachers (Dearing 1994). That is, at Key Stage One and Two, teachers should concentrate on literacy, oracy, numeracy and information technology skills. The report reiterates the importance of a sound foundation by saying: '. . . if children do not leave primary school with a firm grasp of the basic skills of literacy and numeracy, with an appetite for learning and with a belief in themselves and their talents, their future progress will inevitably be stunted' (Dearing 1994: 18).

This is a sound but challenging objective given the range of individual backgrounds, different starting points and consequent needs of pupils in primary schools. It is the class teacher's job to make sure that all children are given equal access to these fundamental skills to facilitate their entitlement to the 'whole' curriculum. Alternatively a reductionist approach to the curriculum, by definition, can only reduce opportunities, particularly for those with complex needs. This will result in children being increasingly afforded status and acceptance (or rejection) through exam success and social conformity. The implications of this for us as a society are profound. This is particularly true if one believes that: 'The schools of the country are its future in miniature' (Hsieh 1948).

The cross-curricular themes contain ideas and strategies which enable the widest range of children to learn how to take responsibility for themselves and how to make choices in preparation for adult life. For this reason their importance in the curriculum needs to be asserted, otherwise we are in danger of replicating and even compounding inequalities of the past.

Since the Audit Commission/HMI Report, *Getting the Act Together* (1992), LEAs have been advised to devolve responsibility and resources for pupils with SEN from the centre to the schools. LEAs are now required to consider schemes which provide funds for pupils with 'special needs' based on 'published rules and principles' (Audit Commission/HMI 1992: 2). It is also recommended that LEAs 'take action to reallocate staff and other resources in line with the trend for an increasing proportion of pupils to be educated in ordinary, rather than special schools' (ibid.: 3). Whereas in the past Tom may have found himself propelled towards the special school sector, there are signs that mainstream schools may be in a better position in terms of resources to respond to individual needs. Whether LEA policies promote this and whether schools choose to do so remains to be seen. Much will depend on the philosophy which underpins thinking about where needs are likely to be best met and what education is ultimately for.

Who establishes needs? Encouraging pupil participation

How are needs to be established? The authoritarian nature of the education system which has governed children's schooling has already been referred to. There are signs however, that authoritarianism within the system is gradually being eroded.

This is largely due to the influence of the Children Act 1989, which has introduced fundamental changes in the legislature governing child care. One of the central themes embodied in the Act is the notion of the entitlement of children to voice their opinions about a wide range of matters in relation to their care, including some aspects of their educational needs. The Act was designed to influence procedures and practices which are predominantly the responsibility of Social Services, however there is a stress on the importance of inter-agency cooperation in all matters affecting the welfare of the child. Education features as an important dimension in any child's life, but reference is made in the Children Act specifically to those children in care or those in need. This aspect of the Children Act resonates with the needs of children who might be described as having 'special needs' and may account for the inclusion of new clauses in the *Code of Practice on the Identification and Assessment of Special Educational Needs*, which is part of the Education Act (Department for Education 1993).

Five stages are specified in the Code and at certain points in the process teachers are required to collect evidence from the child about their personal perceptions of their difficulties and how they would like to address them (DFE 1994a: 24). This aspect of legislation, with detailed implications for teachers, is unprecedented and reflects a more enlightened view of the importance of taking children's views about their schooling into account. The Act states that all state schools must have regard to the Code of Practice from 1 September 1994. This means schools should consider what the Code of Practice advises when drawing up their policies and practice for children with 'special needs'. The Code contains a staged approach to meeting 'special, educational need', where the degree of support matches the level of need. Under the 1993 Act, as under the 1981 Education Act all 'maintained schools must use their best endeavours to make provision for pupils with special educational needs' (DFE 1994a: ii).

This means that while schools will be able to respond in differing ways, they must all have specific policies with regard to 'special educational needs' which will specify:

- the teacher who has responsibility for special educational needs in the school (sometimes called the 'special educational needs' coordinator);
- the schools' mechanisms for the identification and staged support of pupils with 'special needs';
- the strategies for promoting parental involvement.

There is general advice about involving pupils throughout the Code.

The Code of Practice and involving the child

The following is taken *verbatim* from the Code of Practice (DFE 1994a). While it refers exclusively to actions regarding the Code, it has relevance to less formalized classroom practice:

Involving the child

The effectiveness of any assessment and intervention will be influenced by the involvement and interest of the child or young person concerned. The benefits are:

- **practical** – children have important and relevant information. Their support is crucial to the effective implementation of any individual education programme;
- **principle** – children have a right to be heard. They should be encouraged to participate in decision-making about provision to meet their special educational needs.

Schools should therefore make every effort to identify the views and wishes of children about their current and future education. Positive pupil involvement is unlikely to happen spontaneously. Careful attention, guidance and encouragement will be required to help pupils respond relevantly and fully.

Young people are more likely to respond positively to intervention programmes if they fully understand the rationale for their involvement and if they are given some personal responsibility for their own progress. Schools should, for example, discuss the purpose of a particular assessment arrangement with the child, invite comments from the child and consider the use of pupil reports and systematic feedback to the child concerned. Many children with special educational needs have little self-confidence and low self-esteem. Involving children in tracking their own progress within a programme designed to meet their particular learning or behavioural difficulty can contribute to an improved self-image and greater self-confidence. Schools should consider how they:

- involve pupils in the decision-making process;
- determine the pupil's level of participation, taking into account approaches to assessment and intervention which are suitable for his or her age, ability and past experiences;
- record pupils' views in identifying their difficulties, setting goals, agreeing a development strategy, monitoring and reviewing progress;
- involve pupils in implementing individual education plans.

(DFE 1994a: 14–15)

But how can we prepare children to feel they have the right to express their views? How can we give children, particularly those with greatest needs, the confidence and skills to articulate their ideas and feelings?

According to HMI (1990) in their review of the teaching of language and literacy only half of the children surveyed at the age of 11 could argue a point convincingly. Children who are described as having 'special educational needs' are amongst those whose language skills are least developed and who are most at risk of being unable to articulate their needs, ideas and points of view (Bloom and Lahey 1978).

The Speakers Commission on Citizenship (1990) identified a range of intellectual and social skills which they deemed necessary to address issues of rights and responsibilities in encouraging citizenship. These included skills of oral and written expression, making judgements and identifying bias and discrimination. Enfranchising children into decisions about their schooling is inextricably connected to preparing them for citizenship. However, it presents teachers of pupils with complex needs with many challenges. Research conducted by Minkes *et al.* (1994), reviewing the effect on services during the first year of the Children Act 1989 revealed that: 'Increased consultation with young people and their attendance at planning meetings has still to be matched by the skills to ensure genuine participation' (Minkes *et al.* 1994: 18).

A growing body of work reflects the perspective that children deserve to be heard and their views taken seriously (Cox 1991; Keys and Fernandes 1993). Minkes *et al.* (1994) and Wade and Moore (1994) have provided some useful strategies for gathering information from pupils with complex needs. Specific reference will be made to their findings under the section 'Individual assessment: the pupils' views' on page 35.

Facilitating participation

Throughout this chapter we have referred to pupils with 'special educational needs' (acknowledging the limits of such a concept), however we are not arguing from a standpoint of differential teaching for certain pupils or groups, rather, we believe that the adoption of flexible teaching and learning styles and relevant content can benefit all pupils. If teachers examine their practice in order to tailor it to the needs of individual pupils, it can only be a positive benefit to all pupils in their class or school. All pupils have individual needs, wants and aspirations and focusing of policy and practice on the issues which affect them gives everyone the chance to participate and succeed.

Lipman's philosophy

One method for facilitating and encouraging participation for all, a more open and reflective ethos as well as more efficient thinking, is based on the work of Matthew Lipman (1980). Lipman's work has two fundamental aims:

- to foster reasoning skills;
- to create a climate of trust and openness.

Lipman's approach was originally based around seven novels and accompanying teacher manuals. They are designed for the primary age phase upwards and focus on the meanings and ambiguities of words. Most important however is the learning environment in which these materials are to be used. Ground rules are very specific:

- a 'non-judgemental, non-authoritarian and anti-doctrinal' environment should be established;
- pupils should be encouraged to express their views on what they are interested in rather than what the teacher imposes on them;
- teachers are to encourage and guide pupils' talk and indicate to them what they say makes *them* think (that is, teachers must attach importance to what children say and treat them as equals).

This approach is in accordance with and reflects a school environment where active participation for all pupils can be practised, as it can be argued that reason is essential to the maintenance of a civilized community.

Lipman's view is that all pupils have the same educational need, the need to develop the intellectual tools by which they can understand and master the world around them. To be truly autonomous it is necessary to define the terms of our own existence – define our aims, not fulfil the aims of someone else. He says that what happens in many schools is that the children with greatest needs are given the 'basic skills till it comes out of their ears and that does not solve their problems at all' (quoted in Minnes *et al.* 1990: 37). Lipman feels that the basics have consistently failed to deliver, what children with 'special needs' or disadvantaged circumstances require is education of 'unparalleled excellence'; a system of intensive care which includes a strong element of teaching the fourth R; reason itself. The Lipman approach is one example of democratizing classroom interactions, however, the cross-curricular themes offer alternative strategies.

If we look at Tom and his classmates, we can illustrate with some practical examples how these may be applied. One of the first objectives for the teacher is to raise Tom's self-esteem, as well as working towards a positive group identity and mutual respect. This will provide the basis for a lot of the activities which are part of cross-curricular delivery, giving children the skills and confidence to take part in discussions and decision making. By getting children to probe ideas, justify their beliefs and clarify their thinking we are ensuring they become less prone to prejudice, indoctrination and uncritical action.

If children learn to be critical about decisions in their own lives, whether to persist when discouraged, or to listen to friends exhortations to misbehave, we are then preparing them for full and effective participation in society. They are more likely later to be critical in their decisions regarding whether to stay on at school, change school or to try drugs. Systems which are democratized, which enfranchise children throughout are less likely to end up being confrontational and litigious. Schools and local authorities can play a central role in enfranchising children in all aspects of their schooling by using strategies contained in the cross-curricular themes to inform classroom practice in general. The next section looks at specific strategies for doing this.

Learning about individual needs

One approach which can be employed is to ensure that pupils are taught about individual needs and are given some understanding of the position of people labelled as having 'special educational needs'. As one of the cross-curricular dimensions, equal opportunities should be reflected in all aspects of education, but it is also an area which teachers can overtly explore with pupils as part of their personal and social education.

There have been many studies into the development of attitudes, in children from the age of 3 upwards, towards disability and differences in peers (for example Donaldson 1980; Fenrick and Peterson 1984). Many researchers have been concerned to change these attitudes through social and educational integration. Eposito and Peach (1983) studied integration and interaction between pupils with SEN and pre-school peers. They concluded that through regular meetings 'non-handicapped' children developed realistic perceptions of and improved attitudes towards their peers with SEN. Whilst the children with 'special needs' benefited by modifying and improving their social behaviours.

Since the 1981 Education Act there has been an increase in the numbers of schools which have become involved in integration projects with local special schools with the aim of fostering mutual respect and understanding and a shared expertise. Studies by Lewis and Lewis (1987; 1988) found that children's attitudes towards pupils with severe learning difficulties were still forming at around ages 6–7 years. Therefore there is some evidence that discussing SEN with pupils and fostering links with special schools may help pupils to better understand and appreciate the individual needs of others and to cope with those difficulties if they encounter them themselves. This also has a beneficial effect in respect of individual growth and development and formation of attitudes in adult life. What children learn through personal experience can be further enhanced and developed by using teaching strategies which encourage an awareness of self, the group and the diversity of society.

The following represents a range of activities which have been used in a variety of contexts to stimulate such an awareness.

Self-awareness / self-esteem activities

Aims: To give pupils an awareness of themselves and their strengths and weaknesses; To build individual confidence and group trust.
Resources: *Health for Life* 1 and 2 (Health Education Authority 1989), for information and ideas. A booklet for each pupil, 'Images of Me' From *Self Esteem: A Classroom Affair* (Borba and Borba 1982). Paper, coloured pens/pencils, pins, blank of a shield (coat of arms).
Timing: The first two activities would need up to two hours to compete fully with pupils who have moderate learning difficulties.

Activity 1: What am I good at?

- Start with a large sheet of paper divided into four or eight squares, depending on the ability of the group.
- Ask pupils to draw pictures to represent things they are good at or things they enjoy.
- This makes them think about themselves in all contexts in a positive light.
- Share the finished posters with the whole group and discuss ideas and images. How difficult is it to think of things you are good at?

- Emphasis should be on group respect and trust; try to avoid negative responses to individual answers. What everyone has to say is equally important.
- Pin the posters on the wall as a statement of pupils' positive value.

Activity 2: What do others think of me?

- Each person has a sheet of A4 paper pinned to their back. Everyone has a different coloured felt pen. This activity could be carried out in small groups.
- Discuss the importance of positive statements; anything from 'nice hair-cut' to 'good at maths'.
- Then everyone has to write something positive about each other on the paper on their backs.
- Remove the paper and let each person read their own privately. How do they feel about what is written about them? Are they surprised or especially pleased about any comments?
- Pin the papers up next to the work from the previous activity. Have other people picked out the same things about individuals as they did about themselves? Discuss similarities and differences.

Activity 3: Personal coat of arms

- Discuss what a coat of arms is and what it shows about a person.
- Give each pupil a blank coat of arms. Get pupils to divide the shield into quarters. The idea is to fill each quarter with a representation of something which would identify the individual as different from the group. This can be anything from a personal skill to a family trait.
- More able pupils can be stretched by adding a motto at the bottom which sums up the person's aim in life or something they think is important, such as 'be kind and helpful', 'work hard', 'be healthy', 'be happy'.
- Keep the coats of arms anonymous. Hold up each one and discuss what it shows. Can the group identify individual shields?

Activity 4: Honesty card game

- A set of cards needs to be made with statements such as: 'I would like to ...; The best thing that happened to me was ...; Something I am really good at is ...; I work best when ...; I look forward to ...'. The statements can be tailored to suit a particular group.
- Shuffle the cards and put them face downwards in the centre of a table around which the group should all be sitting.

- Pupils pick up a card and read out what it says, i.e. 'I enjoy . . .', 'My favourite food is . . .'.
- Pupils should be encouraged to complete the sentences as honestly as they can.

Activity 5: 'Images of me'

- This is a booklet which encourages pupils to think about themselves and their feelings such as what makes me happy or sad, my friends, my family. It may need adaptation for more able pupils.
- Pupils are encouraged to work individually to fill in their own book. Ideas may be shared with the whole group if appropriate.
- The activity can be completed at home with the help of parents or guardians. This helps to personalize the individual's booklet and may encourage parents to discuss ideas with pupils. Pupils need a photograph of themselves for the front cover.

Pupils may now be more willing to accept each other's strengths and weakness and to be open to different ideas and perspectives. This can then be built on by structuring activities so that everyone can take part and have something to offer.

Individualized assessment: the pupils' views

Another dimension of getting pupils to become more self-aware and articulate their ideas is through more individualized, self-assessment. At Stage 1 in the Code of Practice teachers are required to gather from the child 'personal perceptions of any difficulties' and 'how they might he addressed' (DFE 1994a: 24).

However, as already mentioned, good teaching and learning is based around ensuring pupils feel ownership of decisions with regard to learning objectives. How might teachers with young and potentially vulnerable pupils elicit their views and sensitize themselves to pupils' perceptions of learning needs? In order to gain as rich a picture as possible of pupil needs, the child's perspective needs to be asserted. The following is not an exhaustive list but is intended to provide prompt questions.

Questions for guidance

- What does the child think about themselves as a learner? Do they think they are really good or really bad at certain tasks and, if so what are they?

- What are they interested in and keen to do; e.g. computer games, football, painting?
- What are they motivated by? Parental approval, teacher praise, peer approval or more tangible rewards such as stars, stickers or certificates?
- What is their view of themselves as a member of the class/school? Do they have any special friends? Are there any children whom they do not like? Why?
- In what kind of context does the child learn best? Do they like working on their own, with a partner, in a group or being taught as part of the whole class?
- Do they work better in the mornings or afternoons?
- Do they prefer dominantly visual, auditory or kinaesthetic approaches? That is, when work is presented in pictorial form, when they listen and discuss, when they have to read, or when they have to solve problems by building or creating.
- How do they feel about going out to play at break and dinner times? Is it fun and anticipated with pleasure or simply endured?
- How do they feel about the teaching and other staff? Do they find them approachable, friendly and helpful?
- Do they look forward to coming to school?

The nature of data gathering from pupils will depend on many variables from the effects of the ethos of the school, the relationships between adults and pupils within that context and the inherent characteristics and qualities of the pupil concerned.

Wade and Moore (1994) in their research with children with a wide range of special needs, used a questionnaire/structured interview and sentence completion format supplemented by individual tape recordings, group discussions and children's writing. It is suggested that the place for and the pace of data gathering be determined by the pupils. Minkes *et al.* (1994) urge a flexible interview format from written responses to full verbal or simple yes/no answers. In their research some questions were presented in pictorial or photographic form. Importantly they suggest that interviews are best conducted by someone well known to the child but not directly involved with that particular service (in their case school staff were used to assess the care service). Schools may also wish to consider whether another trusted person, for example a classroom assistant, school secretary or older pupil might elicit more frank responses.

Care needs to be taken not to lead the child; careful listening and watching of non-verbal communication may be most revealing. It may be that in this kind of situation where trust and attention is focused, that the child discloses sensitive information. In such circumstances, teachers need to be aware of procedures relating to child protection (Maher 1987). The child's views can be used in conjunction with other sources of information to evaluate learning needs, assess progress and take appropriate action.

Records of achievement

Another way in which children can be actively involved in constructing and evaluating their progress is through records of achievement. These are usually based on as wide a remit as possible of the child's 'capabilities and skills, and/or understandings, and/or learning experiences, personal qualities and development' (Lloyd-Jones *et al.* 1986: 141).

Records of achievement may contain both formative and summative information about academic and other personal achievements. Children record and evaluate what they have accomplished and set themselves or negotiate new goals. Records are formative in that they help children become reflective and thus gain insights into their strengths and needs by talking and listening to others. They are also summative in that they provide evidence of personal and academic growth. The 'Record of Achievement' folder is the child's property and should reflect their personality and interests inside and outside school. It may contain factual information about academic and social gains such as SATs results and swimming certificates as well as photographic, video and audio evidence demonstrating the processes and products of achievement (for example, the child playing an instrument or making a model).

For the child who is following a behaviour management programme, self-monitoring against a time line of objectives may be included in the folder. Targets for behaviour can be set and the child can then assess how well they have done. This can be done with smiley/sad faces as well as written commentary. For a child with complex difficulties, celebrating each small success is very important, as it may represent a great deal of effort on the child's part (Lewis 1991).

There are numerous ways in which children can take responsibility for evaluating their achievements and identify future goals through records of achievement (see SEAC 1990). This fits well with cross-curricular themes and dimensions, as it links ultimately with helping children become capable and taking responsibility for themselves. Records of achievement also become part of the data base on which to plot a pupil's progress over time and may prove to be invaluable at any stage in learning including the Code of Practice's assessment arrangements.

What are the implications for teachers?

The Dearing Report (1994) has officially recognized the burden under which primary school teachers have been working. It recommends, a slimming down of the curriculum to an essential core in each subject which should allow teachers up to 20 per cent of the timetable to use at their discretion. This flexibility, in theory, allows teachers more time to concentrate on differentiating activities so that all pupils can participate at a level suited to their individual needs. This will be enhanced by the emphasis put on the basic skills of literacy, oracy, numeracy and information technology. These are primarily communication skills and will help to facilitate work on records of achievement and review and guidance, as well as traditional curriculum areas. This emphasis on communication skills will also facilitate the introduction of pupil participation in all aspects of their schooling and life in general as focused by the Children Act (1989) and the Code of Practice (DFE 1994a). These are areas of the utmost importance to all pupils, but particularly those experiencing difficulties, whether they have an official statement outlining their 'special educational needs' or not.

The population of pupils with mild, moderate or specific learning difficulties has also been recognized by Dearing. It is now possible for pupils to work on levels from lower key stages without recourse to a statement, or modification of the curriculum. It is also planned that some recognition of pupils' achievements however small will be given, so that they are not 'working towards level 1' for their whole school career. This will allow other methods of accreditation to be used and will be further helped by the fact that assessment by teachers will have equal weight to SATs when reporting to parents.

All of these recommendations will give teachers the opportunity to reassess their priorities and to put individual children's needs at the centre of their planning, teaching and assessment.

Conclusion

Schools are a key arena where children can reflectively develop knowledge about themselves and their skills and abilities in participating with others. Such development represents a gradually broadening wedge of social awareness and responsibility. Putting children's needs at the centre of school's policies, asserting the importance of good relationships and listening to children's views are all ways in which schools can respond to meeting the widest range of needs as well as help prepare children for responsibilities as citizens. This is also linked with good practice as research on school effectiveness shows these factors to be some of the key determinants of effective schools.

In this chapter we have tried to emphasize the importance of these factors in facilitating participation for all pupils. We have given examples of activities which can help to enhance self-esteem and build group trust. We have also tried to impart the importance we attach to, and strategies for, taking careful account of pupil's views about their learning.

All children, with the widest range of abilities and aptitudes, need to engage in critical dialogue about themselves in their community. 'If we are to encourage children to become responsible and independent we must give them opportunities to display responsibility and independence' (Bertram 1989: 22). We would like to encourage all teachers to recognize the potential for increased pupil participation in individual and communal learning. In this way, it is hoped, more reflective, tolerant and confident school populations, and ultimately, adult citizens will develop.

References

Ainscow, M. and Tweddle, D. (1988) *Encouraging Classroom Success*. London: Fulton.

Alexander, R.J., Rose, J. and Woodhead, C. (1992) *Curriculum, Organisation and Classroom Practice in Primary Schools: A Discussion Paper*. London: HMSO.

Audit Commission/HMI (1992) *Getting the Act Together: Provision for Pupils with Special Educational Needs*. London: HMSO.

Bertram, T. (1989) Communication and the young child: the affective dimension in relationship with adults and peers. *Early Years*, 9(2): 21–4.

Bloom, L. and Lahey, M. (1978) *Language Development and Language Disorders*. New York: John Wiley & Sons Inc.

Booth, T. (1994) Continua or chimera? *British Journal of Special Education*, 21(1): 21–4.

Borba, M. and Borba, C. (1982) *Self Esteem: A Classroom Affair*. San Francisco, CA: Harper and Row.

Brighouse, T. and Tomlinson, J. (1991) Successful schools, *Education and Training Paper No. 4*. London: Institute for Public Policy Research.

Burgess, R. (1983) *Experiencing Comprehensive Education*. London: Methuen.

Campbell, R.J. and Neill, S.R. St. J. (1994) *Curriculum Reform at Key Stage 1: Teacher Commitment and Policy Failure*. London: Association of Teachers and Lecturers.

Corrigan, P. (1979) *Schooling the Smash Street Kids*. London: Macmillan.

Cox, M.V. (1991) *The Child's Point of View*. London: Harvester Wheatsheaf.

Cullen, E. (1994) *Successful Schools for All*. London, National Union of Teachers.

Dearing, Sir, R. (1994) *The National Curriculum and its Assessment* (the Dearing Report). London: National Curriculum Council.

Department for Education (DFE) (1994a) *Code of Practice on the Identification and Assessment of Special Educational Needs*. London: HMSO.

Department for Education (DFE) (1994b) *Special Educational Needs: a guide for parents*. London: HMSO.

Department of Education and Science (DES) *Education Act 1944*. London: HMSO.

Department of Education and Science (DES) *Education Act 1981*. London: HMSO.

Department for Education (DFE) *Education Act 1993*. London: HMSO.

Department of Education and Science (DES) (1978) *Special Educational Needs*, (Warnock Report). London: HMSO.

Department of Education and Science (DES) (1991) *The Parent's Charter – You and Your Child's Education*. London: HMSO.

Department of Health (1989) *Children Act 1989*. London: HMSO.

Donaldson, J. (1980) Changing attitudes towards handicapped persons: a review and analysis of research. *Exceptional Children*, 46(7): 504–14.

Edwards, J. and Fogelman, K. (eds) (1993) *Developing Citizenship in the Curriculum*. London: Fulton.

Eposito, B.G. and Peach, W.J. (1983) Social interaction of exceptional and other children in a mainstreamed pre-school setting. *Exceptional Children*, 49(4): 361–3.

Fenrick, N.J. and Peterson, T.K. (1984) Developing positive changes in attitude toward moderately severely handicapped. *Education and Training of the Mentally Retarded*, 19(2): 83–90.

Fulcher, G. (1989) Integrate or mainstream? Comparative issues in the politics of these policies, in L. Barton (ed.) *Integration: Myth or Reality?* London: Falmer.

Hargreaves, D.H. (1967) *Social Relationships in a Secondary School*. London: Routledge and Kegan Paul.

Health Education Authority (1989) *Health for Life*, Books 1 and 2. London: Nelson and HEA.

HMI (1990) *Aspects of Primary Education: The Teaching and Learning of Language and Literacy*. London: HMSO.

Hsieh, T. (1948) Chinese Epigrams Inside and Out Proverbs. China, reprinted in E. Cullen (1994) Successful Schools For All, *Education Review*, June: 27–30.

Keys, W. and Fernandes, C. (1993) *What Do Students Think About School? Report For The National Commission On Education*. Slough: NFER.

Kyriacoù, C. (1986) *Effective Teaching in Schools*. Oxford: Blackwell.

Lacey, C. (1970) *Hightown Grammar: the school as a social system*. Manchester: Manchester University Press.

Lewis, A. (1991) *Primary Special Needs and the National Curriculum*. London: Routledge.

Lewis, A. (1993) Primary School children's understanding of severe learning difficulties. *Educational Psychology*, 13(2): 133–45.

Lewis, A. and Lewis, V. (1987) The attitudes of young children towards peers with severe learning difficulties. *British Journal of Developmental Psychology*, 5: 287–92.

Lewis, A. and Lewis, V. (1988) Young children's attitudes, after a period of integration, towards peers with severe learning difficulties. *European Journal of Special Needs Education*, 3(3): 161–71.

Lipman, M. (1980) *Philosophy in the Classroom*. Philadelphia, PA: Temple University Press.

Lloyd-Jones, K., Bray, E., Johnson, G. and Currie, R. (1986) *Assessment from Principles to Action*. London: Macmillan.

McNay, J. and Ozga, J. (1985) *Policy Making in Education: The Breakdown of Consensus*. Milton Keynes: Open University Press.

Maher, P. (ed.) (1987) *Child Abuse: The Educational Perspective*. Oxford: Blackwell.

Mason, M. and Rieser, R. (1994) *'Altogether Better': From 'Special Needs' to Equality in Education*. London: Hobsons Publishing plc.

Minnes, F., Overell, G. and Sutton, A. (1990) *The Transformers: The Art of Inspired Teaching*. London: BBC Books.

Minkes, J., Robinson, C. and Weston, C. (1994) Consulting the children: interviews with children using residential respite care services. *Disability and Society*, 9(1): 47–57.

Mortimore, P., Samons, P., Stoll, L., Lewis, D. and Ecob, R. (1988) *School Matters: the Junior Years*. Wells: Open Books.

Office of Population Censuses and Surveys (1989) *Census 1989*. London: HMSO.

OFSTED (1993) *Special Needs and the National Curriculum 1991–92: The Implementation of the Curricular Requirements of the ERA*. London: HMSO.

Palmer, C., Redfern, R. and Smith, K. (1994) The four P's of policy. *British Journal of Special Education*, 21(1): 4–6.

Rosen, M. (1994) Comments broadcast on 'Any Questions?' BBC Radio 4, 11 June.

Rutter, M., Maughan, B., Mortimore, P. and Ouston, J. (1979) *Fifteen Thousand Hours: Secondary Schools and their Effects on Children*. London: Open Books.

SEAC (1990) *Records of Achievement in Primary Schools*. London: HMSO.

Sinclair Taylor, A. (1995) 'Less better than the rest', perceptions of integration in a multi-ethnic special needs unit, *Education Review*, 47(3).

The Speakers Commission on Citizenship (1990) *Encouraging Citizenship*. London: HMSO.

Thomas, G. and Feiler, A. (1988) *Planning for Special Needs: A Whole School Approach*. Oxford: Blackwell.

Tisdall, E.K.M. (1994) Why not consider citizenship?: a critique of post-school transitional models for young disabled people. *Disability and Society*, 9(1): 3–17.

Tomlinson, S. (1982) *A Sociology of Special Education*. London: Routledge and Kegan Paul.

Troyna, B. (1993) *Racism and Education: Research Perspectives*. London: Routledge.

Wade, B. and Moore, M. (1994) *Experiencing Special Education: What Young People With Special Needs Can Tell Us*. Buckingham: Open University Press.

Warnock, M. (1994) Crack the code for the vulnerable 20 per cent. *Times Educational Supplement*, 30 September.

4 IRAM SIRAJ-BLATCHFORD

Racial equality education: identity, curriculum and pedagogy

Editors' introduction

In considering the effects of both the hidden and overt curriculum on children's understanding of racial equality issues, Iram Siraj-Blatchford examines the role of the National Curriculum. She argues that the National Curriculum as it stands has limited potential in promoting racial equity or the education of the whole child. She assesses the impact of racism on children's identities and examines the role of school teachers in promoting a curriculum which is truly accessible to all children. The value of multi-cultural and anti-racist policy formulation and staff awareness is explored in the light of current expectations of OFSTED inspections of school equal opportunities policies. Iram examines the contribution of critical pedagogy and suggests that it may provide a helpful vehicle for teaching in a more democratic way, making full use of the children's everyday life experiences.

Introduction

In this chapter I argue that primary school teachers need to approach issues of racial equality in the classroom from a range of directions. As well as drawing on the current literature in the field, this chapter is also influenced by my experience as a classroom teacher and as a teacher educator working with students and with practising teachers.

The chapter explores the 'multi-cultural' dimension of the national, and whole, curriculum in the context of how children form, and are affected by, their 'racial' identities. Like Debbie Epstein in Chapter 5, I wish to stress the complex nature of identity-formation. The effects of gender, class and other identity-forming categories overlap, in often very complex ways, to form individuals. While the chapter will not focus in detail on this complexity it is important for practitioners to be aware of the nature of shifting and changing identities so that no group of children or individual is essentialized and treated as having a homogeneous experience with others of their 'type'.

My intention is to explore the way in which the multi-cultural and anti-racist components of primary education have been affected during the development and implementation of the National Curriculum. I argue that we need to understand this in order to take our schools forward in racial equity practice and policy. The chapter identifies the importance of the whole curriculum in promoting equality by focusing on aspects of the overt and hidden curriculum, including the role of policy formulation. Special emphasis is given to the role of the teacher as 'critical' pedagogue in the process of empowering children to understand, and respond appropriately, to the differential power often associated with ethnicity and racial groupings.

Racial identities

There is now a great deal of research evidence of racial inequality, at a structural level in education (DES 1985; Troyna 1987). At other levels, such as racial identity, culture and agency there is only an emerging literature, and most of this has been about secondary school children (Mac an Ghaill 1992; Gillborn 1988). This omission is particularly interesting because issues of gender and class identities have received some attention over the years (Willis 1977; Mahony 1985), but it is in the field of cultural studies that most writing on racial identity has occurred and this has mainly been in the areas of media studies and literary criticism. Only very recently has the focus turned to education, but again this has been largely focused on older children or students in higher education.

There has, nevertheless, been some passing recognition in British education of identity as an important concept for bilingual and ethnic minority children. The link has been made between language, culture and identity. For instance, the Swann Report (DES 1985: 3) stated that 'membership of a particular ethnic group is one of the most important aspects of an individual's identity – in how he or she perceives him or herself and in how he or she is perceived by others'. This statement is not elaborated further, or analysed, in the whole body of the report. There is no recognition of the fact that the 'whole' child may be racialized in more than one way. Stuart Hall (1992), for example, discusses not only the discourses of identity but also those of 'difference' within ethnic groups. In the very act of identifying ourselves as one thing, we are simultaneously distancing ourselves from something else. In terms of 'race' and ethnicity, Hall argues that there are contradictions within these categories as well as between these and other categories such as sexuality, class and disability. The way we perceive identities is very much shaped by how they are produced and taken up through the practices of *representation* (Grossberg 1994).

In the same way that Debbie Epstein makes metaphoric use of a kaleidoscope in understanding identity based on a range of inequalities, Bailey and Hall (1992) argue that there will be differences within any identity-forming category, such as 'race'. As they put it: 'black signifies a range of experiences, the act of representation becomes not just about decentering the subject but actually exploring the kaleidoscopic conditions of blackness' (Bailey and Hall 1992: 21). Grossberg (1994) also argues that this notion of the 'kaleidoscopic conditions of blackness' is related to a 'distributive map of the social terrain' where difference is (re)created depending on how and where one is situated in this social terrain (Hall 1992: 16).

Although many teachers may feel overwhelmed by some of this theorizing on identity and difference, I feel that it is important to highlight the complexity of identity formation in children, in order to illustrate, for example, why every black child or every girl child will not perceive themselves in the same way. In fact, children from different structurally disadvantaged groups may often hold contradictory positions, which is why we might find in our classrooms black and other ethnic minority children who are very academically successful in spite of the structural, cultural and interpersonal racism in society. Similarly, we will find working-class boys who are caring and unaggressive and African Caribbean boys who are able and well behaved. The sexism, racism and other inequalities in our society can explain why at a structural level certain 'groups' of people have less power while others have more. But at the level of agency we should beware of stereotypes and focus on individual people. This is not to suggest that we ignore structure; far from it, we need to engage in developing the awareness of children and staff through policies and practices which explain and counter group inequalities. Teachers need to work from a number of standpoints to fully empower the children in their care. As has already been discussed in Chapter 3, children need to be educated to deal confidently and fairly with each other and adults in an unjust society (see also Siraj-Blatchford 1992).

The National Curriculum – where is the 'race' equality dimension?

There are very few books that deal with the practice of racial equality in the primary years. A few have been published in recent years (Cole 1989; King and Reiss 1993; Siraj-Blatchford 1994) but the main emphasis has been on policy and on providing evidence that racism and discrimination exist in education.

The former National Curriculum Council (NCC) originally provided a brief for all subject working parties to include the consideration of issues of racial and gender inequality in their deliberations. The products of the subject working parties varied in their commitment to providing teachers with the relevant non-eurocentric content they would need to plan for multi-cultural and anti-racist approaches. Limited but useful components were included in the English, science and design and technology orders. These were further complemented with the arrival of the eight cross-curricular guidance documents. Most multi-cultural and anti-racist educators tried to be optimistic and set about attempting to make the best of the windows of opportunity made available by these limited innovations.

However, some important events have occurred in the last five years which have caused an erosion in the multi-cultural and anti-racist potential of the National Curriculum. This is by no means a coincidence but represents a concerted and deliberate effort to put equality issues on the back burner. These changes occurred at a time of right-wing attacks on equality measures across the board – in schools, LEAs and in teacher education. Public statements have been made by government ministers, including John Major (1992) claiming that social justice education has resulted in adverse effects upon the teaching of 'basics'. These opinions have not been based on research evidence but rather what Kate Myers (1990) has described as 'equiphobia', an irrational hatred of those who strive for social justice and those on the political left.

In 1989 the NCC set up the multi-cultural task group consisting of nine experts in the field of multi-cultural education. The group met for over a year and produced a report based on the remit given by the NCC to provide teachers with guidance on how to develop the multi-cultural component of education. The report was never published and Sally Tomlinson (1993), one of the task group members, has written a detailed account of the events that led to non-publication. She explains that:

> Opposition to multi-cultural and anti-racist curriculum development thus became, during the 1980s, a right-wing political tool for encouraging a populist belief that such development threatens the nation's heritage and culture and erodes educational standards. With this kind

of opposition it should not be surprising that those who believe that multi-cultural developments are in fact intended to produce a just, decent, humane education system, have found difficulty in making their views prevail.

(Tomlinson 1993: 26)

The reasons for non-publication still remain unclear.

As the National Curriculum subject documents have been revised many of the multi-cultural statements have been removed. Further erosion in equity education could also be linked to the demise of power of the local authorities associated with the local management of schools. Racial equality provision has become particularly vulnerable for children in mainly white locations where many teachers have yet to realize its vital importance and others stand isolated. The other main victims are bilingual children whose teachers often have little training on the delivery of the National Curriculum or appropriate assessment procedures with children learning English as an additional language. The cutbacks in Section 11 funding have exacerbated the situation further for many ethnic minority children and their teachers. Not surprisingly schools have generally been more concerned with the assessed components of the curriculum than with the cross-curricular elements.

However, even in the face of such change some educationalists remain optimistic. A working group of teachers, heads and academics met over the two years up to April 1993 at the Runnymede Trust in London, led by the director Robin Richardson, to produce guidance for schools on racial equality. The document has been published under the title *Equality Assurance in Schools* (Runnymede Trust 1993) and provides guidance to schools for incorporating racial equality at all key stages in all the national curriculum subject areas. It pays particular attention to issues of management, organization, governors and parents, and will be helpful to any school as a starting point for developing racial equality practice and policy. Teachers should be aware that the multi-cultural dimension of the curriculum is an accepted and legal entitlement for all children, as laid down in the Education Reform Act (DES 1988). In spite of the significant erosion in the National Curriculum of the multi-cultural components there are still spaces for action and committed teachers can still find some grounding for their good practice. As Anna King (1994: 3) suggests:

However inadequate, muddled or attenuated NCC references to multi-cultural education may be, the documents can be used collectively to justify and assert the importance of the pluralist approach, and it can be argued that those working for anti-racist, multi-cultural and global approaches to the curriculum now have considerable statutory and non-statutory support.

King goes on to provide, like the Runnymede Trust document, a detailed account of where in the published NCC documents we will find reference to multi-culturalism as a cross-curricular dimension which teachers are expected to put into practice.

Since the merger of the NCC with the Schools Examination and Assessment Council (SEAC) to form the Schools Curriculum and Assessment Authority (SCAA) another set of problems has arisen. Research was beginning to show clearly that the weighty and over-burdened National Curriculum was unworkable for teachers and children in the limited time available to schools and Sir Ron Dearing was given the task of reviewing the curriculum and assessment arrangements in consultation with teachers (SCAA 1994). Many people in schools, LEAs and teacher education were already familiar with the problems. In teacher education I often had students who returned from teaching practice to report that their teacher and school were unable to implement the multi-cultural dimension because they were too busy with the National Curriculum. Teachers clearly needed the multi-cultural task group's guidance on the implementation of this cross-curricular dimension while at the same time the statutory orders were being revised and, slowly but surely, these revisions omitted the references to other cultures or non-eurocentric knowledge.

The SCAA consultation exercise resulted in a slimming down of the National Curriculum, which is both good and bad news for racial equality practice; more time is available to incorporate the cross-curricular elements, but many teachers still feel the National Curriculum is over-prescriptive. The Dearing review has had little to say about the cross-curricular components, and as a result teachers remain unclear about the status of these components. No initial or in-service teacher education has been planned to develop teachers' understandings of the racial equality issues. The only other positive aspect of recent developments is that the Office for Standards in Education (OFSTED) has incorporated as part of all school inspections the need for schools to ensure that they have an equal opportunities policy. However, even this requirement could lead to schools carrying out a 'cosmetic' exercise.

It remains clear that there has been little positive follow-up by the SCAA in this area. The focus in the last two years has been on subject knowledge and content. What has been forgotten is that the real subjects in the education system are the children. Many good teachers still continue to use this as their starting point in order to make the curriculum *relevant* to the children and to produce good learning outcomes. Curriculum knowledge is important, and the main concern of many teachers and parents have is *whose* knowledge it is that is valued and transmitted. Of course every child should learn about books and number. But, if books never present ethnic minority characters positively, or numbers are seen only as the invention of Europeans then children are being misinformed about the potential and the history of achievement of people from other cultures. The full range of multi-cultural and anti-racist educational practices, with appropriate examples, cannot be entered into here, however, readers will find the references for this chapter a very useful source for books containing practical strategies in working with three- to eleven-year-olds and their parents. In the remaining part of the chapter I wish to explore the hidden curriculum and those teaching strategies favourable to racial equality approaches.

Dealing with the hidden curriculum

Racism is pervasive throughout British society and this is reflected in education as much as in other sectors such as employment, housing and the media. It follows that schools alone cannot make a significant difference to structural 'race' inequality in society, but they do have a key role in educating children about why racism exists and why it is wrong. If this is not done the ethos of the school will remain racist, albeit subtly so. According to Giroux (1983: 43) the hidden curriculum is a powerful medium by which unstated norms, values and beliefs are: 'embedded in and transmitted to students through the underlying rules that structure the routines and social relationships in school and classroom life'.

There are a growing number of studies which show that children of different ethnic backgrounds experience their education in different ways (see Gillborn 1990; Grugeon and Woods 1990; Wright 1992 and Mac an Ghail 1992). David Gillborn's (1990) study of a comprehensive school shows how South Asian and African Caribbean children experience school. The study highlights the influence of different racial stereotypes and the particularly disadvantaged position of African Caribbean children. Similarly, the work conducted by Grugeon and Woods (1990) and Wright (1992) in the nursery and primary years found that children could not be lumped into a single category of 'black'. Although this term is useful in signifying the experience of racism for particular groups, it is inadequate as a means of identifying the different ways in which children from different ethnic minority backgrounds experience school and racism. This is a complex issue, but teachers should be aware of it, because careful observation of children's experiences in school is still a helpful way of identifying what action needs to be taken.

The experience of the white, ethnic majority group is equally important when addressing the hidden curriculum and racial equality. It is often the education of ethnic *majority* children that is poorly catered for in this area (see Epstein and Sealey 1990; Tomlinson 1990). Their attitudes and behaviours are often the cause of racism and they are racist because they have learned it from others around them.

In order to promote a racial equality *ethos* in our primary schools, an issue which has to be examined if the hidden (and overt) curriculum is to be affected, we have to address the need for a school policy. A policy which looks at racial equality would need to explore every aspect of school life including the curriculum, assessment, organization, management, employment procedures, links with parents and a code of procedure for dealing with racist harassment. Most importantly the issue of staff attitudes deserves significant attention, because as Bagley (1992) has argued after trying to work, with varying degrees of success, with two schools on policy development:

> The general indifference and resistance of teachers towards the development of a multi-cultural policy might also have been provoked by their own personal and professional sensitivity towards 'race' and education as white teachers.
>
> (Bagley 1992: 245)

Many schools begin their policy developments in this area from different angles. For instance, the initiative might have arisen from one member of staff's concern for the re-examination of books and other materials for racial bias or from a specific incident related to racist name-calling or bullying. In the past, external requests from LEAs with multi-cultural or anti-racist policies might have instigated a group of staff to develop their own school policy within the framework of the wider LEA initiative. Nowadays however, the stimulus for developing a policy, especially in mainly white areas, is more likely to come from the expectation of an OFSTED inspection. Whatever the initial motivation for a policy the process of policy development will require staff (including support staff) to work through a number of stages. I have argued elsewhere (Siraj-Blatchford 1994) that schools need to be aware that the policy itself is perhaps less important than the process of writing it and that the phases of implementation are when, some would argue, the 'real' work begins.

Several general stages of policy development can be identified (All London Teachers Against Racism and Fascism (ALTARF), 1984; Siraj-Blatchford 1994) among others that are specific to individual schools. A key member of senior staff should be responsible for coordinating this process, ideally to empower staff to work collectively and with 'ownership' of the process. The following phases deserve special consideration.

Staff knowledge and expertise: an audit is valuable in identifying the strengths and weaknesses. Following this staff might wish to collect resources, videos and materials which promote discussion and increase the awareness of institutional, cultural and personal racism. This knowledge could then be applied to the existing structures and practices within the school to examine some of the taken-for-granted assumptions about 'good practice'.

Learning from others: once an audit of staff and school needs is identified, including the objections to developing racial equality measures, a school is in a stronger position to enlist outside expertise where it is required. The use of books, packs, speakers, children's resources and specialist journals can form a useful focus for further discussion.

Setting an agenda and involving everyone: small groups of staff or the whole staff in smaller primary schools could set an agenda to address key areas of concern. Some of these might include: consulting other schools with policies, resource implications, organization of learning and educational resources, the school environment, parents, governors, curriculum, language, code of practice on racist harassment, assessment and staff appointments.

The process of implementation: when the policy is written it is still only a framework for further practice. It is also a public and overt commitment to providing an anti-racist and multi-cultural service to children, staff and parents. The ensuing change in the practice, procedures, behaviours and structures which might perpetuate racism is the acid test of any policy. This requires a carefully planned monitoring and evaluation exercise on the part of senior management and other staff in a school.

School staff will also need to discuss at which point in the process of policy development they would like to involve parents and children. This is an issue that can be discussed with classes of children or through the school council if the school has one. Efforts should be made to involve the whole school and local community when the staff feel knowledgeable enough to deal with the issues that might arise; for example, racism from parents.

From policy to pedagogy

A critical pedagogy is an appropriate vehicle for the promotion of open dialogue, learning and teaching in classrooms where children are encouraged to behave as 'little citizens' with some social responsibility for their school community. The sort of teaching and commitment required of teachers to develop this practice is partly outlined in Chapters 2 and 10 of this book. However, in order to understand the 'critical' component of teaching Mostern (1994: 256) offers a helpful explanation:

> the critical pedagogue is always someone who teaches from where the student is at, rather than from where the teacher is at. This does not mean that the teacher denies his or her pedagogical intentions or

specific expertise, but merely that s/he respects the myriad expertise of the students that s/he does not share.

Mostern is writing here as an educator of adults, but most early years teachers and indeed many primary school teachers have come to the same conclusion based on research in child developmental psychology. The notion of starting from what children can do rather than from what they can't do is familiar to teachers who prefer to base their teaching on the discourse of 'development' rather than that of 'delivery'. This is not to suggest that teachers should adopt a crude Piagetian model of stages of capability, but that we can start from what the children bring into school or nursery from their lived experience and *extend* and build upon that experience. In this way children can be expected to empathize with the needs and aspirations of an interdependent community within their school and beyond. Age is only important in signifying the *way* a particular concept is taught, rather than whether it is taught or not.

The Runnymede Trust guidance on *Equality Assurance in Schools* (1993) provides a useful plan for the primary curriculum under five main categories. These are: programmes of study; teaching and learning; resources and materials used for learning; assessment and evaluation. The guidance shows quite clearly how all five areas are interrelated and they provide a sound framework for critical pedagogy. In order to promote cultural and linguistic diversity in the curriculum, it is worth revisiting some of the elements mentioned in the Runnymede Trust guidance.

Programmes of Study – the Runnymede Trust Guidance asserts that children should have the opportunity to explore:

- 'aspects of their own and others' personal and cultural identity (e.g. allegiances, religious beliefs, experiences and feelings)
- issues in social and political life (e.g. rights and obligations, power differences, conflicts of interest, justice and fairness)
- values and concerns which humans have in common (e.g. trade, shelter . . . decision-making . . .)'.

(Runnymede Trust 1993: 24)

Through making such explorations children draw heavily on their own and their family's experiences and knowledge about languages, history and the rich heritage of the achievements of different groups of people. In pursuing programmes of study that value diversity and question similarities and differences in human achievement the children are actively engaged in their learning and have some opportunity to negotiate their curriculum with the teacher. The skills, concepts, knowledge and attitudes developed in such work enhance the content and learning of the National Curriculum. Children have to operate proficiently in English and even engage in metalinguistics.

They have to operate as scientists, historians and artists in making decisions and recognizing human achievement, bias, and in interpreting visual and printed images. None of this is beyond the grasp of primary age children.

Teaching and learning strategies: many adults find it hard to work in groups collaboratively, yet we expect young children to do this without giving them the prerequisite skills to cooperate. Working together, listening and showing mutual respect are vital ingredients for groupwork and discussion, especially when sensitive social and political issues are being discussed. Children should have access to a range of learning experiences differentiated according to need. Children who are acquiring English as an additional language should have support within the classroom and plenty of practical experience to develop subject-specific language. Everyone in school needs to be aware of a code of behaviour which respects individuals and groups, regardless of their 'race', gender, economic situation or special need. Wherever possible the school must make use of the children's life experiences in a positive and empowering way. All children should have a regular forum for self-expression through their languages and the arts, and every attempt should be made to provide a balance in terms of the variety of human achievement from a range of cultures in science, technology, literature, mathematics, music, artistic heritage, religious knowledge, sport and the humanities. Teachers might have to make a concerted effort to develop or locate resources which promote the above practice as many of our current resources are biased in favour of Western and European achievement. Parents can be a great source of support but in mainly white areas there may also be some resistance from them and this has to be dealt with as an issue for the whole staff and not just individual teachers (see Siraj-Blatchford 1994).

Assessment: teachers and children see assessment as a normal and important part of the teaching and learning process but school staff need to inform themselves of the danger of bias in standard and teacher assessments. Bilingual and ethnic minority children are particularly vulnerable if assessment tasks are culturally exclusive and based wholly on a child's proficiency in English. Where possible the images presented to children in assessment tasks should reflect their cultural heritage. A non-judgemental approach which avoids stereotyping based on ethnicity, gender and class will probably only be achieved in schools where a good deal of collaborative and critical evaluation of the history of assessment has taken place. A whole school policy is essential and all the planning for racial equality will require regular monitoring and evaluation.

Conclusion

In this chapter I have tried to identify some of the key areas which could be considered by primary schools in the move towards promoting racial equality. I have argued that structural racism is still widespread but that children experience racial inequality in different ways in terms of individual identity, within their ethnic group, and across their whole identity in terms of gender, social class background and ability or disability. I argue that there are several areas that teachers need to explore in order to provide a sound basis for learning for all children. The National Curriculum development and implementation is described as having failed to adequately incorporate the multi-cultural cross-curriculum dimension. Teachers remain bereft of guidance in this area. It is suggested that there are some 'spaces' for the development of good multi-cultural and anti-racist practice, but that teachers will need to show greater commitment to the area. The hidden curriculum is also seen as a vital space for changing school practice through the development of an active racial equality policy through staff development.

Finally, I refer throughout the chapter to a handful of useful resources which teachers can use to support the racial equality dimension of their work. I stress the need for a critical pedagogy which allows children more power in the negotiation of the curriculum with teachers, and which allows for more reference to the children's real life experiences in their day-to-day school work. I draw on the work of the Runnymede Trust (1993) guidance on racial equality and the national curriculum to emphasize some practical teaching strategies which can be adopted in an effort to promote racial equality in all schools.

In the context of racial equality, as in every other, children and their families have their own unique identities, understandings and styles of learning. In this context as much as any other we must recognize that children of a particular ethnic background are not simply a homogeneous group. Just as we cannot assume that all ethnic majority children of the same age have the same understandings of number, so we must not assume that they have developed the very same values towards, and understandings of, difference. Whilst a structural understanding of racial inequality is necessary it is not sufficient in considering the needs of individual children. Our expectations of a group can, all too easily, lead us to disadvantage the individual.

References

All London Teachers Against Racism and Fascism (ALTARF) (1984) *Challenging Racism*. Nottingham: Russell Press.

54   *Iram Siraj-Blatchford*

Bagley, C. (1992) In-service provision and teacher resistance to whole-school change, in D. Gill, B. Mayor and M. Blair (eds) *Racism and Education: Structures and Strategies*. London: Sage Publications in association with the Open University.

Bailey, D. and Hall, S. (1992) The Vertigo of Displacement: shifts within Black Documentary Practices in D. Bailey and S. Hall (eds) Critical decade: black British photography in the 80s. *Ten – 8*, 2(3), special issue.

Cole, M. (ed.) (1989) *Education for Equality: Some Guidelines for Good Practice*. London: Routledge.

Department of Education and Science (DES) (1985) *Education for All*; The Swann Report. London: HMSO.

Department of Education and Science (DES) (1988) *Education Reform Act 1988*. London: HMSO.

Epstein, D. and Sealey, A. (1990) '*Where it really matters . . .*' *Developing anti-racist education in predominantly white primary schools*. Birmingham: Development Education Centre.

Gillborn, D. (1988) Ethnicity and educational opportunity: case studies of West Indian male–white teacher relationships, *British Journal of Sociology of Education*, 9(3): 371–85.

Gillborn, D. (1990) '*Race', Ethnicity and Education*. London: Unwin Hyman.

Giroux, H. (1983) *Theory and Resistance in Education: a pedagogy for the opposition*. London: Heinemann.

Grossberg, L. (1994) Introduction: bringin' it all back home – pedagogy and cultural studies in H. Giroux and P. McLaren (eds) *Between Borders: Pedagogy and the Politics of Cultural Studies*. New York: Routledge.

Grugeon, E. and Woods, P. (1990) *Educating All: Multicultural Perspectives in the Primary School*. London: Routledge.

Hall, S. (1992) Race, culture and communications: looking backward and forward in cultural studies. *Rethinking Marxism 5*: 10–18.

King, A. (1994) Introduction, in A. King and M. Reiss (eds) *The Multicultural Dimension of the National Curriculum*. London: Falmer Press.

King, A. and Reiss, M. (eds) (1993) *The Multicultural Dimension of the National Curriculum*. London: Falmer Press.

Mac an Ghaill, M. (1992) Coming of age in 1980s England: reconceptualizing black students' experience in D. Gill, B. Mayor and M. Blair (eds) *Racism and Education: Structures and Strategies*. Sage Publications in association with the Open University.

Mahony, P. (1985) *Schools for the Boys*. London: Hutchinson.

Major, J. (1992) Prime Minister's speech at the Conservative Party conference, Brighton, September.

Mostern, K. (1994) 'Decolonization as learning, practice and pedagogy in Frantz Fanon's revolutionary narrative, in H. Giroux and P. McLaren (eds) *Between Borders: Pedagogy and the Politics of Cultural Studies*. New York: Routledge.

Myers, K. (1990) Review of 'equal opportunities in the new era'. *Education, 5*, October: 295.

Runnymede Trust (1993) *Equality Assurance in Schools: Quality, Identity, Society.* Stoke-on-Trent: Runnymede Trust and Trentham Books.

School Curriculum and Assessment Authority (1994) *The Review of the National Curriculum: A Report on the 1994 Consultation*, com/94/118. London: SCAA Publications.

Siraj-Blatchford, I. (1992) Why understanding cultural difference is not enough, in G. Pugh (ed.) *Contemporary Issues in the Early Years.* London: Paul Chapman Publishers Ltd.

Siraj-Blatchford, I. (1994) *The Early Years: Laying the Foundations for Racial Equality.* Stoke-on-Trent: Trentham Books.

Tomlinson, S. (1990) *Multicultural Education in White Schools.* London: Batsford.

Tomlinson, S. (1993) The multicultural task group: the group that never was, in A. King and M. Reiss (eds) *The Multicultural Dimension of the National Curriculum.* London: Falmer Press.

Troyna, B. (ed.) (1987) *Racial Inequality in Education.* London: Tavistock.

Willis, P. (1977) *Learning to Labour.* Farnborough: Saxon House.

Wright, C. (1992) Early education: multiracial primary school classrooms, in D. Gill, B. Mayor and M. Blair (eds) *Racism and Education: Structures and Strategies.* Sage Publications in association with the Open University.

5

DEBBIE EPSTEIN

'Girls don't do bricks': gender and sexuality in the primary classroom

Editors' introduction

For anti-sexist education to be fully realized Debbie Epstein challenges readers to analyse gender inequality within the context of what Judith Butler has described as the 'heterosexual matrix' (Butler 1990). Like Iram Siraj-Blatchford's, the chapter recognizes the discursive nature of inequality with respect to 'race', gender and class, and shows how these may impact cumulatively on children's identities. Based on her own teaching experience in an infant school, Debbie examines a case study of a small group of children's gendered and heterosexist behaviour. She argues that current anti-sexist practice is inadequate and calls for a more effective practice based on an understanding of how 'compulsory heterosexuality' determines our gendered positions.

Introduction[1]

The purpose of this chapter is to explore some ideas about the ways in which children and teachers actively construct discourses of gender and sexuality in primary classrooms and, in the light of these ideas, to raise some questions about current practices in anti-sexist education and about how a more effective anti-sexist practice could be developed. My thinking about these issues arises from my experience as a classroom teacher, a head of infants in a large primary school, a local education authority teacher adviser and, more recently, as a university teacher and researcher engaged in the exploration of issues of equality and in challenging inequalities. While this chapter is specifically about gendered discourses in primary classrooms, it is my view that the varying oppressions experienced by children (due to, for example, age, class inequality, disablism, (hetero)sexism and racism) are intertwined and interembedded.

This is not to suggest that inequalities are experienced in any simple 'add-on' form but rather that they are (re)produced and lived out in specific and contingent ways and that the precise relationships between different forms of inequality are shifting. It might, in this context, be helpful to imagine looking through the lens of a kaleidoscope. The pieces inside the kaleido-scope remain the same as the base is twisted, but the exact configuration of what is seen depends on the specific ways in which the pieces fall in rela-tion to the mirrors and on the intensity of the light in which they are seen. In a similar way, precisely what is seen in any examination of oppression of any kind will depend on the precise focus of the investigation, but each form of inequality shapes and is, in turn, shaped by others. Thus the experiences of girls and women are shaped not only by (hetero)sexism, but also by questions of age, class, (dis)ability, ethnicity, 'race' and so on and, at the same time, gender inequalities shape the ways in which these other differences impact upon people's lives.

It is however extremely difficult, if not impossible, to capture in writing the complexity of the ways in which different inequalities inter-relate and, for the sake of clarity, it is often necessary to treat them as if they were separate. Thus, in a book such as this, we get separate chapters dealing with (dis)ability (Chapter 3), racism (Chapter 4) and gender (this chapter). Nevertheless, I hope that this chapter together with those of the other authors will help readers to think not only about gender inequality and how to combat it, but will also provide a model for the analysis of complex inequalities.

There are several key arguments presented in this chapter: first that sex-ism is, by definition, heterosexist and that sexism cannot, therefore, be understood in the absence of an analysis of heterosexuality as both political and institutionalized; second, and resulting from the first argument, that to be effective anti-sexist education must also be anti-heterosexist; third that school is an important locus for the inscription of gender and of heterosex-uality and that it is, therefore, also an important locus for challenging domi-nant discourses of (hetero)sexism; and finally that children are active in the making of their own meanings and that anti-sexist *intentions* do not always succeed, in part because of the very complexity of social relations noted above and in part because of the inherent difficulty of challenging dominant discourses.

Understanding children's gendered subjectivities

During the summer of 1994 the Commission for Racial Equality ran a billboard advertising campaign which carried the slogan, 'There are lots of places in Britain where there is no racism'. The picture illustrating the slogan was of a line of nude infants, both girls and boys, from various ethnic groups with the word 'here' stamped across their foreheads. The idea underlying this advertisement was, obviously, that infants are not born racist, but learn racism as they grow older. Similarly, it might be said that babies are not born gendered, but learn to become gendered. It is a commonplace in the social sciences that 'sex is biological, but gender is social'. In other words, according to this argument, sex is a given which cannot be changed. Gender, on the other hand, is learnt and the ways in which one becomes gendered may vary according to time, place and culture. I would, in contrast, agree with the arguments of post-structuralist and post-modernist theorists such as Henriques *et al.* (1984), Davies (1989) and Butler (1990) who suggest that biology and culture cannot be separated in this way. What is important, they argue, is *how* biology is understood and interpreted rather than biology on its own. In other words, the fact that boys/men and girls/women nearly always have easily differentiated genitals[2] is less important than what it means to be(come) a girl/woman or a boy/man. As Davies (1989: 12) maintains: 'Genitals do not have to be linked to feminine or masculine subjectivities unless we constitute them that way'. Nevertheless, the idea of human beings as bipolar, biologically sexed opposites is extraordinarily difficult to shake. Most of us experience biological sex as 'real' in ways which are connected to our gender identities and appear to be more fixed than practically any other part of our experience. The questions which need to be addressed are how this becomes the case and what it means for anti-sexist practice in the primary classroom.

Judith Butler (1990) suggests that it is impossible to understand gender except through what she calls the 'heterosexual matrix'. That is to say, the concept of genderedness becomes meaningless in the absence of hetero-sexuality as an institution which is compulsory and which is enforced both through rewards for 'appropriate' gendered and heterosexual behaviours and through punishments for deviations from the conventional or 'norm'. The compulsory character of heterosexuality is perhaps easier to see in the context of adults. Gay men, for example, are literally imprisoned for their consensual behaviour while lesbians frequently lose custody of their children only because of their sexual orientation. Neither gay men nor lesbians are allowed to marry or establish relationships which are legally or socially recognized, while heterosexual men and women have their relationships recognized in law and receive considerable approbation and material reward for them (in, for example, the form of wedding presents and a married person's tax allowance). It is perhaps less clear when thinking about children, mainly because we are not accustomed to thinking about them in terms of sexuality or sexual orientation. But 'inappropriate' gendered behaviour is usually punished either by adults or peer groups (though boys who are 'cissy' are usually punished more severely than girls who are 'tomboys'), while 'gender-appropriate' behaviours are rewarded. I would, moreover, suggest that these behaviours are tied to practising (for) heterosexuality (see Epstein 1993a; Epstein and Johnson 1994).

What this means in practice is that a great deal of social/cultural work goes into maintaining the gender/sex of boys/men and girls/women as binary opposites. A good deal of this work has already been done by children entering nursery classes at the age of 3 or 4 and even more has been done by children starting compulsory schooling at the age of 4 or 5. Indeed, there is much evidence to suggest that children between the ages of 5 and 8 are strongly attached to the notion of more or less stereotypical gender difference as immutable (see for example Paley 1984; Davies 1989; Lloyd and Duveen 1992 see also Millman in this volume). Furthermore, as Lloyd and Duveen (1992: 7) point out:

> By the time children are old enough to begin formal schooling, they already voice occupational preferences which are parallel with adult gender stereotypes. For very young children, gender functions as a conceptual scheme through which other aspects of their social world are assimilated. . . . [By] 2 years of age, children display a gender-marked behavioural preference and play more with gender appropriate toys.

This is hardly surprising, given the insistence with which infants, from birth onwards, are told their gender. Indeed, within developmental psychology it is taken as one of the prime markers of early cognitive development that a child knows which gender it belongs to. It would in these circumstances be astonishing if the vast majority of 3 to 5 year-olds had not inscribed themselves well within the gender to which they had been ascribed. If others constantly interpret them and their world through discourses of gender difference, what else is available to infants as they begin to make sense of the world for themselves? And, of course, this is true even in the most anti-sexist of households, for there is no language other than the language of gender available. Parents may dress their girls in 'boys' or 'unisex' clothes, they may buy their boys dolls (other than action men) and their girls Lego, but they have no choice about ascribing a gender to their children, talking about them and to them in gendered ways, using gendered pronouns and so on. When one hears a mother talking to a young baby, for example, she will regularly refer to the infant in a gendered way – 'Who's a good girl/boy, then?' – and it is difficult if not impossible to imagine a parent being able to avoid gendering the ways she or he addresses her or his child. Furthermore, even if the parents were to achieve a relatively gender-neutral home environment, the baby cannot but swim in a sea of gendered discourses, already in place at the time of the child's birth, for gender is one of our primary ways of making sense of the world.

The point of Judith Butler's (1990) argument about the need to understand gender and, by inference, children's attachment to stereotypical gendered difference through the 'heterosexual matrix' is that limits of what is permissible for each gender are framed within the context of compulsory heterosexuality. It is clear, for example, that the meanings of being both a 'good girl' and of being a 'real boy' are constituted within a silent heterosexuality, which is made all the more powerful by its very silence (see also Epstein and Johnson 1994). Clarricoates (1978: 156) for example, in her germinal work on primary school teachers and children, offers the following quotes from teachers:

> ... the girls seem to be typically feminine whilst the boys seem to be typically male ... you know more aggressive ... the ideal of what males ought to be.

> I think the boys tend to be a little more aggressive and on thinking about it the male is the same in the animal world ... we are animals basically.

Clarricoates' paper is concerned with the gendered ways in which teachers treat children and the gendered ways that children behave, having learnt their gender 'appropriate' sex roles. However, nowhere does she point out that these roles are not simply about the genders of the children but also about the assumed heterosexuality of those genders. Being 'typically feminine', for example, does not make sense except in a heterosexual relationship to the 'masculine'. Equally, the notion that 'boys tend to be a little more aggressive' is clearly tied to discourses of the male sex drive (see Hollway 1984, 1989), which assume that men, being 'naturally' more aggressive, will take the lead in sexual encounters with women and have strong needs for (instant) gratification of their sex drive.

Although Clarricoates' paper is now quite old, it still has purchase and influence on the way teachers think about anti-sexist education and many later discussions have been not dissimilar from hers, either in their findings or in their analysis of them (see, for example, Paley 1984; Browne and France 1985). Even in those works which acknowledge the importance of heterosexism in the construction of gender relations in schools (for example Askew and Ross 1988; Lees 1993), this aspect receives little attention. However, as Askew and Ross (1988) point out, the most virulent terms of abuse used by boys against each other from a very young age are those which carry the connotation of gay sexuality ('poof', 'cissy', 'wimp') while, as Rogers (1994) points out, the term 'lezzie' is experienced by girls as being even more damaging than the term 'slag' (that is, it is worse not to be heterosexual than it is to be 'overly' heterosexual). What these terms of abuse have in common is that they are used not just as a way of policing sexual boundaries but also of punishing those whose behaviours are perceived as being not sufficiently masculine or feminine. Boys are not called 'poof' only because or when they identify as gay, but also (and indeed more frequently) when their behaviour appears to be 'feminine'. Likewise, the term 'lezzie' is used for girls who appear to be too 'aggressive' or 'assertive' (especially in relation to boys) as well as for those who openly identify as lesbian. Furthermore, as my own observation shows, these terms of abuse are in regular use in primary and even infant playgrounds as well as in secondary schools.

It is within a theoretical framework which understands sexism as (hetero)sexism that I now wish to turn to the analysis of classroom interactions and initiatives.

Gender in and across the curriculum

Nearly all the curriculum guidance published by the National Curriculum Council (NCC) called for schools to provide for gender equality. Indeed, the whole notion of a common curriculum for all pupils up to the school leaving age has long been one which many feminist educators have supported. However, the NCC has not provided any clear guidance as to *how* the desire for equal opportunities might be transformed into forms of practice which result in equality. As Riddell (1992: 231) has pointed out:

> If such discussion does not take place, then it is very likely that parents, teachers and pupils will both deliberately and unconsciously subvert the idea of a common curriculum, so that divisions based on gender, race and class continue to exist in both the overt and covert curriculum.

The concept of equality contained within the National Curriculum can be characterized as falling within a basic equal opportunities paradigm. This model assumes that doing the same subjects, with the same formal curriculum content, will be enough to create equality. In other words, equal access to the formal curriculum is everything and differences in social context are ignored. However, children in different social groups do not start from the same place. Neither do they have the same experiences of schooling, for their lives are mediated through inequalities relating to (at least) class, ethnic group and gender. The National Curriculum thus offers a much weaker version of equality in education than do the various anti-racist and anti-sexist initiatives which have taken place during the 1980s (see for example Askew and Ross 1984; 1988; Epstein and Sealey 1990; Epstein 1993b; Minhas 1986). Typically, these suggest ways of challenging stereotypes, of providing 'positive images' and of trying to change the 'hidden curriculum'. The assumptions underlying such approaches include: that there is no 'level playing field' and that equal access is therefore a necessary but not a sufficient condition for the achievement of equality in education; that social justice and anti-discriminatory practice are important and that we have to look not only at the content of the curriculum, but also at the mode of teaching and the hidden curriculum overall.

As early as 1981, Valerie Walkerdine suggested that matters were more complicated than either liberal, equal opportunities versions or most anti-sexist versions acknowledged and that children were active makers and producers of sexist meanings (Walkerdine 1981). More recently, her work has been taken up by Bronwyn Davies (1989, 1993) who has explored the ways in which children take up gendered positions in schools and, in particular, how they can make sense of anti-sexist stories in ways which may 'rescue' these stories from feminist interpretations and re-inscribe them in sexist discourse. The way in which I understand the anti-sexist work which I have done in schools owes much to my reading of Walkerdine and Davies (as well as to my observations of the children involved in the work). Most of the rest of this chapter is devoted to the exploration of an anti-sexist initiative I undertook with young children which could, I believe, be used as a starting point for developing more effective anti-sexist work.

Some of my critique of my own work arises from the fact that I now consider it to have been somewhat over-simplistic. This was, in part, the result of my not having previously thought through the relationships between gender and compulsory heterosexuality or between sexism and heterosexism, and that the initiatives I undertook (along with virtually all other initiatives that I know about) had not developed their anti-sexism within the framework of an overall critique of compulsory heterosexuality. The story of this particular initiative will illustrate three things: first, that children are active agents in making their own meanings and in (re)constructing sexism; second, that certain kinds of work can, to a more or less limited degree, shift children's positionings within sexist and heterosexist discourse and third, that the ways these initiatives both do and do not cause such shifts raises issues for the development of a progressive, anti-sexist curriculum. Such curriculum development needs to be in dialogue with both the successes and failures of any previous initiative and previous strategies must be interrogated if we are to move on. Such an interrogation is the purpose of the rest of the chapter.

'Girls don't do bricks'

As I have argued above, children are active makers of meaning. This is not simply a question of socialization, which carries with it the idea that the way we behave and how we become who we are is effectively predetermined by a society which is somehow separate from us. However, this is not the case. We create ourselves through our interactions with our environment. As Davies (1993: xvii) puts it:

> ... children [are] not ... pressed into masculinity and femininity as sex role socialisation theory puts it. Rather, in learning to be coherent members of their social worlds, they ... actively [take] up their assigned gender as their own in ways not necessarily compatible with the ways teachers and parents [tell] them gender should be done.

In other words, children do not have completely free choices about the ways they behave or the people they become but they are, nonetheless, active agents in their own self-creation. This is not just a question of 'learning *by* doing'. Rather, it might more accurately be said that doing *is* learning.[3] Consequently, when children play in gendered ways they are actively creating themselves as gendered, learning to interpret and understand the world in the same moment as they are playing and indeed changing their immediate world by their play. What this means in practice is that children will not simply accept alternative meanings offered them by feminist or anti-racist teachers – although these may well provide alternative discourses for those seeking them (see also Davies 1989, 1993; Troyna and Hatcher 1992). They need to be able to act on the world in alternative ways in order to be able to experience it differently.

An opportunity to facilitate such alternative experience was presented to me, as a teacher of a year 1 class, when three girls, Clare, Becky and Natasha,[4] came to see me with a complaint: they were being prevented from playing with the large bricks by Michael, Nathan and Ben. Furthermore, said Clare, 'Michael says girls don't play bricks. If I want to play in the bricks I must be a boy!' Clare was extremely upset, more by the accusation of being a boy than by being denied the chance to play with the bricks (though she wanted to do that as well). She clearly felt that being told she must be a boy was one of the worst insults that could be thrown at her and perhaps this is not surprising in the light of young children's attachment to gender difference (and in the light of the intended insult). The girls did not wish to be labelled as boys but they did, quite vehemently, wish to play with the bricks.[5]

Rather than simply telling the boys off for their behaviour or trying to distract the girls (both actions which a busy teacher might well adopt for good reasons), on this occasion I decided to discuss the matter with the rest of the class. I called a 'circle discussion', in which all the children took part, and asked the three girls and the three boys to explain their positions to the class. Clare, Becky and Natasha said that they wanted to play with the bricks but that the boys were mean and would not let them. Michael, Nathan and Ben said that the girls only wanted to spoil their buildings, an accusation which the girls hotly denied. Eventually (and conventionally in anti-sexist practice) I suggested that it might be fair for girls to have regular times during which they could play with the bricks, since most of the time it seemed that the boys had the bricks to themselves. The children agreed to this – although some of the boys were not too happy about it and expressed their unhappiness by taking every opportunity to reclaim the bricks for their own use. Lloyd and Duveen (1992: 69) recount a similar event in a classroom they observed:

> On one occasion, social category membership was invoked success- fully by girls in order to gain play resources for their own sex group. The teacher reluctantly agreed to organize turns for boys and girls after complaints about boys monopolizing the big blocks. One of the boys tried to re-establish the rights of boys by pointing out that the girls were not using them at the moment, but the girls remarked sharply that boys were not allowed to play with the blocks at that time; it was the girls' turn.

In my class there was a period when only Clare, Becky and Natasha chose to use the bricks during the girls' time (though they chose to use them with remarkable tenacity). However, gradually other girls also began to take the opportunities offered them to play with the bricks. Although the initial 'buildings' were rather tentative, the girls gradually developed styles of building which involved using the different shapes and colours available to them in complex ways. Some of their play involved creating domestic situations; they would sometimes, for example, build a 'house' in order to introduce dolls into it and play domestic games. However, the bricks were not 'given'. In order to achieve domestic play, the girls had, perforce, to do some building and the more familiar they became with this activity, the more it seemed to interest them.[6] Within their domestic play, girls could adopt 'feminine' roles which had reference to future heterosexual expecta- tions of marriage and motherhood. At the same time they could and did build complex structures with the bricks. Girls could, then, at one and the same time position themselves firmly as feminine and do the supposedly 'masculine' activity of building – thus giving the lie to the notion that 'girls don't do bricks' and to the idea that they must be 'boys' if they wanted to play in this 'inappropriately' gendered way.

Another strategy used by the girls to maintain their positioning as feminine was the invocation of fairy tale fantasy play. For example, on one occasion Becky and Jenny began their play as follows:

Becky: Let's build a house. Come on.
Jenny: Yes, let's. Then we can make tea . . .
Becky: (*interrupting*) Not a house, a palace. The dolls can be princesses.
Jenny: Princesses, mm.
Becky: It'll have to be big.
Jenny: Big and grand.

The two girls then began a building which took them the best part of an hour to construct and during the course of this time they were joined by two other girls. Each time one of them suggested that it was time to 'play princesses', one of the others proposed a new and more magnificent extension to their 'palace'. It is interesting to note that this was not simply the result of a more dominant girl getting her way, for the person making the suggestion for improvements differed each time and the other girls entered enthusiastically into the task of further building. When it came to clearing up time, the girls were still engaged in the construction of their large and complicated 'palace'. They were, justifiably, proud of it and of their skills as builders and wanted the whole class to see their building. The 'palace' was much admired by all and the next day Michael dictated his diary as follows:

> I used to think girls don't do bricks. Then we made a girls' time for bricks. They made really good houses, specially Clare. Now I like to play with Clare in the bricks. We make lots of good buildings.

What is interesting here is not only that Michael chose to write this but that, as far as I could observe, Michael and Clare did not play together with the bricks or, indeed, anywhere else in the class. The point is not to question Michael's 'honesty' here, but that, whether or not he actually played with Clare, doing so had now become an object of desire for him.

From being one of the prime leaders of the boys' faction which did not want the girls to be allowed to play with the bricks, he had become both admiring of their activities and desirous of their company (at least in theory). In view of the ways in which, from an early age, girls and boys generally separate themselves firmly in play and of the contempt which these particular boys had previously expressed for girls' abilities to undertake 'masculine' activities, this was a significant shift.

The experience of those girls who took advantage of the girls' only time to play with the bricks helped them to do and learn a number of things which were subversive of stereotypical femininity: first, they experienced success at doing traditionally boys' activities; second, they became more confident and adept at these activities, developing spatial and technological abilities usually associated with masculinity and third, they found that they could be assertive and challenge the boys' domination of particular areas of the classroom. The fact that the girls positioned themselves firmly as girls (by using domestic and fairy tale narratives in their play) while at the same time challenging stereotypical femininity may be seen as being in some ways contradictory. However, this is a problem only if we see people as being in some way unified, monolithic (and rational) wholes. But people (girls and boys, women and men) do occupy contradictory positions within discourse. Identity is not whole and unchanging, but is, rather, constantly (re)created within particular discursive fields (like schools) and from available discursive positions. Indeed, it is this that gives some hope for successful anti-sexist (and generally anti-oppressive) practice. In this particular case, the girls' ability to challenge (both for themselves and for the boys) gendered stereotypes was made possible precisely *because* they were able to occupy contradictory positions at the same time, playing with the boys' toys while taking up feminine subject positions. In this particular experience, the girls were no longer placed in a polar position of femininity (in which everything they did had to conform to 'girlish' behaviour) but could behave in girlish ways at the same time as adopting some of the characteristics and possibilities of being a boy which they themselves had identified as desirable.

Conclusion: implications for practice

In analysing the events which took place in my classroom during this initiative I have drawn on insights which I did not have at the start of the work. My decision to allow the girls time on their own with the bricks was, as pointed out above, drawn from conventional anti-sexist practice of the time. My view was that allowing the girls time on their own would help them to develop their confidence and would, at the same time, destabilize sexist stereotypes about what girls could and could not do – and of course this did, in part, happen. What I did not anticipate was that this would take place at the same time as the girls positioned themselves firmly within discourses of femininity which reinscribed conventional, (hetero)sexist gendered relations. This meant that I did not take the opportunity to reflect with the girls (or indeed the boys) on what the meanings of these discourses were.

It is my contention here that it is not possible to 're-socialize' children into anti-sexism (or anti-racism) since they are active producers of meaning through discourse on their own account. However, the discourses they produce will, inevitably, relate both to the discursive field within which they find themselves and to the discourses with which they are familiar and comfortable and through which they can recognize themselves. By definition, all discursive fields have within them a number of different and usually contradictory discourses and the struggle is over which particular discourses within the field (and, therefore, ways of understanding the world) gain and maintain hegemony. More specifically, schools and classrooms constitute discursive fields within which meanings are produced about social relations of many kinds (including, particularly, age, class, gender/sexuality and race). The discourses in play will include and be drawn from those current in the world outside the school – whether they are dominant (and oppressive) or oppositional (and anti-oppressive) – and their relative strengths will depend on the previous experiences of the children and teachers, on the organization of the classroom and on the particular micro-politics of the school (see also Ball 1987, 1990; Epstein 1993b).

What can the anti-(hetero)sexist teacher do in this context? The very act of being anti-(hetero)sexist introduces alternative discourses into the classroom. Furthermore, because of the specific age relations of schooling and because of our common-sense understandings of what it means to be a teacher, what the teacher thinks, says and does will have a powerful influence on the discursive field (especially where children are young and have not yet become invested in opposition or resistance to schooling). However, attempts simply to tell children to be more anti-sexist or to resocialize them into anti-sexism are, as I have argued throughout the chapter, doomed to failure. What is needed is the introduction of activities and organization of the classroom in such a way that alternative and oppositional discourses and discursive practices are available to the children.

In introducing a girls-only time to play with the bricks I inadvertently allowed a space within which the girls could both hold on to their (presumed heterosexual) femininity and challenge stereotypes of what it means to be a girl. What I did not do was allow them the time or space to reflect critically on their own activities. Young children may not do this in precisely the ways that adults might, but, as the example above shows, they are able from a very young age to think critically about what is and what is not allowable in a given, concrete situation. If, for example, I had asked the girls why they kept on building their magnificent palace, instead of stopping to play princesses much earlier, they would probably have discovered that they enjoyed the actual act of building. This could have led to further (but unpredictable) discussion about why they needed to retain the princess fantasy narrative (rather than, for example, a narrative about building a garage or a fort) which might have clarified for them their own investments in femininity, a prerequisite for working to change those investments. At the same time discussion with the boys about their changing perceptions of what girls could or could not do (and about the desirability, *qua* Michael, of playing with them) might also have helped shift the classroom discursive field more than I actually managed to do. The key, here, is in creating and providing classroom materials and curriculum content which both necessitate activities which run contrary to heterosexist gendered stereotypes *and* which allow the children to remain comfortable in their play with their current (but developing) understandings of what it might mean to be a boy or a girl.

Notes

1 I would like to thank Iram and John Siraj-Blatchford for their editorial work on this chapter (and especially for their patience in waiting for its completion!). I would also like to thank Judith Green, Peter Redman and Deborah Lynn Steinberg for their helpful comments on earlier versions of the chapter.
2 Although it is sometimes difficult to distinguish between 'girl' and 'boy' genitals at birth and sometimes babies have a gender ascribed to them which is later changed. It is also the case that 'gender testing' in international competitive sports have revealed several women (with female genitals) who have 'male' chromosomes (male athletes have never been tested for gender).
3 I am grateful to Judith Green for her help with these paragraphs and, in particular, for this formulation.
4 All names have been changed in order to retain anonymity.
5 For a comparison with the work described here, see Davis and Tichner (1986) and Brown (1990).
6 This is in contrast to the girls in a different class, and on a different occasion, when I created a girls' time to play with the toy cars. Here, since the cars were simply there, ready for use, the girls entered very quickly into domestic fantasy and did not emerge from it (see Epstein 1993b for a fuller description).

References

Askew, S. and Ross, C. (1984) *Anti-sexist Work with Boys*. London: ILEA.
Askew, S. and Ross, C. (1988) *Boys Don't Cry: Boys and Sexism in Education*. Milton Keynes: Open University Press.
Ball, S.J. (1987) *The Micro-politics of the School: Towards a Theory of School Organization*. London: Methuen.
Ball, S.J. (1990) *Politics and Policy Making in Education: Explorations in Policy Sociology*. London: Methuen.
Brown, C.A. (1990) Girls, boys and technology. *School Science Review*, 71(257): 33–40.
Browne, N. and France, P. (1985) Only cissies wear dresses: a look at sexist talk in the nursery, in Weiner, G. (ed.) *Just a Bunch of Girls*. Milton Keynes: Open University Press.

Butler, J. (1990) *Gender Trouble: Feminism and the Subversion of Identity*. London: Routledge.

Clarricoates, K. (1978) Dinosaurs in the Classroom: a re-examination of some aspects of the hidden curriculum in primary schools, reprinted in M. Arnot and G. Weiner (eds) (1987) *Gender and the Politics of Schooling*. London: Hutchinson/Open University Press.

Davies, B. (1989) *Frogs and Snails and Feminist Tales*. St Leonards, NSW: Allen and Unwin.

Davies, B. (1993) *Shards of Glass: Reading and Writing Beyond Gendered Identities*. St Leonards, NSW: Allen and Unwin.

Davis, J. and Tichner, J. (1986) Can girls build – or do they choose not to? A study of girls and boys using construction materials, in *Primary Teaching Studies*, 1. London: Polytechnic (now University) of North London.

Epstein, D. (1993a) Practising heterosexuality. *Curriculum Studies*, 1(2): 275–86.

Epstein, D. (1993b) *Changing Classroom Cultures: Anti-racism, Politics and Schools*. Stoke-on-Trent: Trentham Books.

Epstein, D. and Johnson, R. (1994) On the straight and the narrow: the heterosexual presumption, homophobias and schools, in Epstein, D. (ed.) *Challenging Lesbian and Gay Inequalities in Education*. Buckingham: Open University Press.

Epstein, D. and Sealey, A. (1990) *'Where it really matters . . .' Developing anti-racist education in predominantly white primary schools*. Birmingham: Development Education Centre.

Henriques, J., Hollway, W., Urwin, C., Venn, C. and Walkerdine, V. (1984) *Changing the Subject: Psychology, Social Regulation and Subjectivity*. London: Methuen.

Hollway, W. (1984) Gender difference and the production of subjectivity, in J. Henriques, W. Hollway, C. Urwin, C. Venn and V. Walkerdine (eds) *Changing the Subject: Psychology, Social Regulation and Subjectivity*. London: Methuen.

Hollway, W. (1989) *Subjectivity and Method in Psychology: Gender, Meaning and Science*. London: Sage.

Lees, S. (1993) *Sugar and Spice: Sexuality and Adolescent Girls*. London: Penguin.

Lloyd, B. and Duveen, G. (1992) *Gender Identities and Education*. Hemel Hempstead: Harvester Wheatsheaf.

Minhas, R. (1986) Race, gender and class – making the connections, in *Secondary Issues: Some Approaches to Equal Opportunities in Secondary Schools*. London: ILEA.

Paley, V.G. (1984) *Boys and Girls Superheroes in the Doll Corner*. Chicago: University of Chicago Press.

Riddell, S.I. (1992) *Gender and the Politics of the Curriculum*. London: Routledge.

Rogers, M. (1994) Growing up lesbian: the role of the school, in D. Epstein (ed.) *Challenging Lesbian and Gay Inequalities in Education*. Buckingham: Open University Press.

Troyna, B. and Hatcher, R. (1992) *Racism in Children's Lives: a Study of Mainly-White Primary Schools*. London: Routledge in association with the National Children's Bureau.

Walkerdine, V. (1981) Sex, power and pedagogy. *Screen Education*, 38: 14–24.

6

ALISTAIR ROSS

Children in an economic world: young children learning in a consumerist and post-industrialist society

Editors' introduction

Here, Alistair Ross argues that the NCC curriculum guidance (CG4) provides an outdated and conservative basis for educational provision in economic and industrial understanding (EIU). He cites a wide and impressive range of research evidence and provides a challenging view of an alternative approach that is grounded in the realities of children's own experiences and understandings.

Alistair argues that it is the role of the educator to help the child make sense of their social environment rather than to filter out (or in) particular experiences. This is a theme that is revisited throughout this book. As John Holt (1984) argued, children *are* inescapably active, constructive members of our community. We actually ignore this at their peril, and perhaps at humanities' peril, as enduring attitudes and values are otherwise formed by our children in contexts that we fail to acknowledge or simply ignore.

Alistair identifies the essentially capitalistic basis of the curriculum guidance offered, and in doing so recognizes that education is essentially ideologically driven. For any educationalist to claim otherwise would be to present the dominant ideology uncritically. Capitalism provides just one (perhaps transitory) economic system. Socialism provides another and other forms are equally possible. Our education system should not indoctrinate children into either of these dominant systems, nor into any other systems. The best protection from any such abuse, and at the same time a sensible application of sound educational principles, would be to base provision on children's own existing knowledge. We can then help them to make sense of these economic systems in their own ways. This way, they will eventually be able to locate their own position in relation to the various traditions.

Introduction

The first cross-curricular theme to be introduced was launched in the spring of 1990, when the National Curriculum Council (NCC) published *Curriculum Guidance 4: Education for Industrial and Economic Awareness* (CG4) (NCC 1990). The reactions in the popular press linked this theme to Thatcherism, and broadly welcomed what it saw as an attempt to instil the virtues of capitalistic enterprise in the young. Reaction elsewhere was suprisingly muted. Perhaps most of the teaching profession were too much caught up in the emergence of the history and geography National Curriculum documents, as the final reports of the working parties in these two foundation subjects were published in the same month. Duncan Graham (1993) saw the struggle for the publication of the cross-curricular themes as one of the most significant of his Chairmanship of the National Curriculum Council: he introduced this theme as 'an essential part of every pupil's curriculum ... needed in all key stages' (NCC 1990: i). Many primary teachers, it seems, rejected this assertion, not only because the introduction of cross-circular themes represented yet another impossible curriculum demand, but also because it threatened the apolitical assumptions of much of the existing primary curriculum. The argument that the document represents an unnecessary political intrusion into the curriculum, as an example of neo-liberal economic propaganda, needs to be examined.

But it is equally important to examine the evidence of how children do learn about economic and other social activities. Whatever the imperatives and directives of the NCC document, there are many examples and studies that show that young children are acutely aware of how the society about them manages (or fails) to conduct its affairs. This includes the ways in which we organize such core social activities as work, how we exchange goods and services, how we ascribe value to activities and to items, and to the distribution of wealth. Children live in a world that is controversial. (Carrington and Troyna 1988) and deserve to be introduced, through their education in schools, to strategies that will enable them to understand it.

Many radical teachers might add that schooling should empower children to take control.

This chapter offers a critical but constructive approach to the development of economic and industrial understanding in schools. It argues that CG4 presents an essentially conservative and dated view of economics. Its presentation of the ways in which industry is constructed and managed and of the ways in which economic affairs are conducted is an essentially nostalgic view of Britain's industrial and economic heritage. It has plausibly been argued (Wiener 1981) that the British education system, and the wider social system of which it is part, have developed an anti-industrial culture over the past century that has belittled the industrial success that has led to the nation's wealth, disparaging work in industry, and thus damaging economic development. But even if this were true (and it has been contested; see Ahier 1988), CG4 propagates the economic values of the 19th and first half of the 20th centuries, and is unlikely to develop either the economic attitudes or the industrial knowledge necessary for the early 21st century.

It will also be argued that the kind of economic education and understanding of industry that should be developed in primary children's schooling is radically different from the neo-classicist monetarism described in the CG4. In a highly consumerist society, children need to develop a highly developed critical faculty towards the market's creation and manipulation of consumer needs. In a society that cannot find employment for all its citizens – yet still links status, power and privilege to certain types of employment – children need to develop sensitivities and values geared towards a post-industrial society. This is a society in which it is predicted that 90 per cent of the new jobs created will be filled by women, and children will need to consider gender roles in this new light. In a world in which resources are being used at an ever-increasing rate to the detriment of both the local and the global environment, children will need to learn how to rationally consider the forces currently demanding economic growth. And in a world of gross economic inequality between north and south, children will need to consider if their generation will be able to manage a better redistribution of wealth.

All of these issues, of consumerism as a form of capitalist manipulation, of work and employment in post-industrial society, of gender roles in the workplace, of limited global resources and of environmental degradation and of the distribution of wealth in a global context, are economic questions, but ones that hardly figure in CG4. They are all questions that will need to be considered when the children now passing through school are adult citizens. They are therefore questions which demand curriculum attention now.

Curriculum Guidance Four

But CG4 does not address these issues, and the development of economic and industrial awareness within the curriculum over the past twenty years, particularly that of the primary school curriculum, give reason for apprehension about whether it is capable of addressing them.

The specific expectations of children at Key Stage 2 (8–11) reveal the NCC's assumptions about the kind of economic understanding that is being aimed at:

1 Understand some of the implications of limited resources
2 Know that all decisions involve opportunity cost
3 Be aware of some of the costs and benefits of everyday economic choices; recognise that people can have different and conflicting interests
4 Appreciate that human needs, unlike wants, are universal and recognise that for many people needs are not met
5 Understand what it means to be a consumer and how consumers and producers relate to each other
6 Understand how money is used in the exchange of goods and services and know some of the factors which affect prices
7 Understand that workplaces are organised in different ways
8 Have some understanding of how goods are produced, distributed and sold
9 Know about public services, shops, offices and industries in their local community; understand the importance of these to local people
10 Develop their understanding of the nature of work and its place in people's lives
11 Develop an awareness of the part played by design and technology in industrial production
12 Be aware of some effects of new technology and the implications for people and places
13 Appreciate some of the environmental and social issues associated with economic and industrial activity
14 Recognise similarities and differences between economic and industrial activities in different parts of the world.

(NCC 1990: 21–4)

Comparing the equally prescriptive lists for the other three Key Stages, it is possible to construct a set of threads that develop economic and industrial ideas over the 5 to 16 age range, resulting in the necessary 'knowledge' that 'competition between business enterprises promotes efficiency of production', that 'efficient use of resources in producing goods and services created wealth for individual enterprise', and that the basic principles of setting up a business include efficient management (NCC 1990: 40–1). Though there are other statements, many of which are less politically loaded and which would have more widespread acceptance, the overall impression of CG4 is twofold:

- it represents an attempt to construct an ideologically-driven enterprise culture, in which the individual and their duties and responsibilities are emphasized at the expense of society and the rights it affords individuals, through the school system, and
- it represents a 'top-down' model of curriculum development, in which younger children are prepared for the upper secondary school subject of economics (in its most 'classical' form).

There are other possible objections to the inclusion of economic and industrial understanding in the curriculum: there is the argument that developing such work in the primary school detracts from childhood innocence. Some hold that primary schools should present an essentially protected view of the 'real' world, in which things that adults find contentious, uncomfortable or disputatious are avoided. More generally, it is widely acknowledged that the primary school curriculum has been overloaded with detailed curriculum provisions (for example Thomas 1993). More fundamental problems with economic and industrial understanding arise from the essentially abstract nature of many of the concepts with which it deals. Economics is a conceptual subject: a simple scanning of the list of Key Stage 2 objectives above reveals concepts that are difficult enough for many adults. The work of developmental psychologists such as Jean Piaget (1965) would suggest that children in the primary phase of education are unable to handle any of these ideas at the level of abstraction necessary for them to be meaningful. Applying Piaget's model to the teaching of social studies with primary-aged children, McNaughton (1966: 26), for example, argues that 'most primary children will not, without considerable prompting, stand back from what they read about people to compare them with others and with themselves'. Such arguments might be supported by some teachers and other adults, with casual evidence that they have not observed children discussing economic or industrial ideas, or expressing much interest in the economy or the world of work. Eclectic observations may be cited to support the view that primary-aged children do not understand these areas, but they reflect the traditions of classroom discourse to which the particular children described have become habituated. 'Not in front of the children' attitudes today are as much about money as they were previously about sex. But, for these teachers and adults, children are a-economic and unaware of industrial processes. But economic socialization must, of course, occur at *some* period in our development. Maital (1982: 24) ironically points to the absurdity of denying that growth in economic understanding takes place before adulthood: 'Economic man [*sic*] is an obstetric miracle. From the pages of economic journals he springs to life full blown'.

It is clearly important to ensure that children are not indoctrinated into the practices of inequality that are embedded in the current organization of work. It is not difficult to point to many examples of practices in the workplace that conflict with the equal opportunities policies of many schools and most local education authorities. Many workplaces enshrine racist, classist and sexist practices, and these are evident to children if they tour workplaces: women confined to low-paid light industrial work and to certain kinds of office work; separate dining and lavatory facilities for workers and managers; ethnic minorities largely confined to the lower paid work. It could be argued that simply exposing children to such discrimination can lead them to believe that such practices are inevitable, acceptable and normal. Many of our workplaces are capitalistically organized, and while the astute primary teacher will draw attention to the imperfect levels of equality in the organization of the workplace, few will encourage children to establish industrial ownership, the exploitation of workers, and the extraction of profit from their labour (Campbell 1986). But, taken to its extreme, this again would only expose children to a carefully sanitized view of the world. A final argument against developing economic and industrial understanding in primary schools might be that it is of little practical use. Industry and the economy are fast-moving arenas, and any statements about it now, or sets of transferable skills defined now, are not likely to be valid in seven to fifteen years time, when the children might begin to enter the labour market.

To summarize: industrial and economic understanding for primary-aged children *might* be variously seen as:

- a political intrusion of capitalism – the extension of employer's and capital's hegemony;
- an over-conceptualized area inappropriate for young children's stage of understanding;
- remote from children's experience, or as unsuitable and unethical to be put before the young, and of little practical benefit.

However, it will be argued here that children are far from being the passive recipients of a curriculum constructed for them by adults, of whatever political persuasion or for whatever purpose. They are actively constructing understandings from their experiences; and they have economic experiences in their everyday life, around which they are inevitably making meanings. The task of the educator is to help the child make sense of their social environment, not to attempt to filter out (or in) particular experiences on the grounds of their suitability or relevance.

Do children have experiences of the economic and of the industrial?

Children actually know a great deal about adult work. Hutchings (1993) describes the work that young children see in the home, the workers in the street and in shops that they encounter at an early age. Children also see workers about the school. Additionally, they discuss work with members of their family; Tizard and Hughes (1984) and Dunn (1988) cite many examples of pre-school children's conversations about work and employment, and the economic facts associated with this.

Primary-aged children experience a wide range of industrial and economic phenomena in their everyday life, and they attempt, with varying degrees of success, to make some sense of this, generalizing from the evidence, and sometimes beyond it. Moreover it is important for reasons that are both social and educational that they are encouraged to become critically aware of the economic dimension in their lives. The school shares some responsibility for this. Teachers who deny a place in the curriculum to the development of children's socio-political ideas are rejecting the validity of the many socio-political experiences of everyday life that children bring to school (Harber 1980).

In primary-aged children this knowledge grows and becomes more complex. A whole range of different kinds of work are put before them through television, and in particular through popular soap operas and advertisements. The story-lines of soap operas frequently reflect the work experiences of their characters, and children frequently cite these characters' experiences as contributing to their knowledge of adult economic life. After the writer had had a vivid description from an 11 year-old girl of the various ways of borrowing money to start a business, he asked her how she knew so much:

> *Kelly:* Well, you have to watch all these Dynasty things – they go [moving to a convincing Texan accent] 'I'm going to have to get a loan, Richard – because I can't set up my business without a loan. Will you lend me the money, and I'll pay it back ...' ... they tell you all the things, really.
>
> (Ross 1989)

Hutchings (1989: 1) plots a whole range of work-related concepts and how they develop over the years of primary education. Children are 'not passive recipients who simply absorb what they see like sponges; rather they use all these sources to construct their own ideas. They work out explanations for the things that they see; they make generalizations; they transfer the knowledge they have to other situations; and they make judgements'. These experiences naturally vary from child to child, and the conceptual understanding varies accordingly. Sometimes there can be highly developed understandings of trade. The following transcript of a conversation between the author and a 9 year-old boy in central London illustrates the highly sophisticated sense of price, value, profit and economic necessity that he possesses. It will be of interest to the reader to know that the boy's class teacher described him as having far fewer mathematical and numerical skills than she would expect in a child of his age:

Scott: My dad's got a fruit 'n' veg stall. He borrowed the money from the bank. He paid it back, like two to three days after . . . if he sells it too cheap, you don't get no profit. He works it out, like say a box was five pound, and he gets something like fifty . . . a bag of spuds is seven fifty, and he gets fifty-two pound in a bag. So he would work it out that it would be fifteen or twenty pence a pound, and he would get something like two pound fifty profit.

Interviewer: And what happens if he sells something that goes off, like . . . peaches? And he gets to the end of the day and he's not sold them all?

Scott: If he aint sold 'em all, he'd put the prices down. Cos the peaches would go off. Or he'd take them indoors and he'd put 'em in the fridge. But say they were fifteen pence each, he'd put them down to ten.

Interviewer: How much would he buy them for?

Scott: Maybe – three pound a crate, something like that.

Interviewer: Right, how much is that for each peach?

Scott: I think you get something like twenty-eight peaches [in a crate].

Interviewer: Would he ever sell them for less than he paid for them?

Scott: Only if he didn't sell them – but he would make it back up with the other fruit. It's not worth letting five pound drift off instead of four.

(Ross 1989)

This extract is also interesting because of Scott's working-class origins. Contrast it with this example drawn from Tizard and Hughes' 1984 study of 4-year-old girls with their mothers and in nursery school. In this dialogue, between the middle-class Rosy and her mother, Rosy discusses the fact that the window cleaner who has just called at the house is to be paid. At first she is uncertain as to the direction the payment will go:

Rosy: Then the window cleaner gives it [the money] to us?

Mother: No, we give the window cleaner money, he does work for us, and we have to give him money.

> *Rosy:*   Why?
> *Mother:* Well, because he's been working for us cleaning our win-
>   dows. He doesn't do it for nothing.
> *Rosy:*   Why do you have money if you have . . . if people clean your
>   windows?
> *Mother:* Well, the window cleaner needs money, doesn't he?
> *Rosy:*   Why?
> *Mother:* To buy clothes for his children and food for them to eat.
> *Rosy:*   Well, sometimes window cleaners don't have children.
> *Mother:* Quite often they do.

Later in the day, after the window cleaner has been paid and left, the
mother speculates to Rosy:

> *Mother:* I expect the window cleaner's going to have his lunch now
>   . . . I expect he goes to the pub and has some beer and
>   sandwiches.
> *Rosy:*   He has to pay for that.
> *Mother:* Yes, he does.
> *Rosy:*   Not always, though.
> *Mother:* Mm, always.
> *Rosy:*   Why not?
> *Mother:* They won't give him any beer and sandwiches if he doesn't
>   have any money.
>   (Tizard and Hughes 1984: 120–1)

As Tizard and Hughes point out:

> Confusion about the relationship between work, money and goods
> seemed to be less common among the working-class children. Perhaps
> because their father's work was more clearly related to money, rather
> than the interest of the job, or because with a more limited income
> the arrival of the weekly pay packet was a more important event, the
> relationship between money and work was more often discussed in
> working-class families.
>   (Tizard and Hughes 1984: 123)

Similar evidence is provided in many of Dunn's transcripts (1988), and
similar conclusions are arrived at in Walkerdine (1988) and Walkerdine and
Lucey (1989). It may well be that children like Rosy need extra support
in development in the economic sphere.

   Children's experience is more limited than adults. Nevertheless, children
will actively seek to make sense of their social and economic encounters,
drawing on the limited bank of observations that they do have to construct
an explanation of the new encounter. While many adult reactions to inci-

dents such as Rosy's dialogue may be to focus on the mistakes, to the mis-formulations and seemingly quixotic explanations, what is really the remarkable feature is that there is a very active attempt to arrive at a logical explanation. It is this tendency to generalize from the evidence that they have that is seen when young children describe the use of money in a shop as a ritual exchange. What they see, on nearly every occasion, is the customer passing some money to the shopkeeper, and the shopkeeper passing some money back. Small pieces of paper and piles of small metal coins pass in each direction. Very often, the customer is given more coins than they pass across. So when they are asked why we give money to the shopkeeper, it should be hardly surprising when a 4 year-old responds: 'Because he won't give any money to you if you don't' (Hutchings 1989: 13). Equally, when asked where money comes from, adults may expect to hear an answer that shows that it is (usually) earned. Young children, interpreting the term 'money' literally as coins, often say 'from the shop'. In terms of where coins in our pockets and purses actually come from, this is entirely correct – we rarely collect coins from our workplaces, or from banks and building societies.

Hutchings offers further examples of the ways in which children's powerful generalizations lead to conclusions that defy adult logic. When asked if a shopkeeper will sell an orange for more, the same, or less than he bought it for, many young children said he would sell it for less. When asked why this should be so, the explanation was simple and logical to this 5 year-old: 'Because it's a second-hand orange'. A 6 year-old reasoned, again with some logic, that he would sell it for 'less, because if he gets it from another shop, people might as well get them from that shop'. There is a powerful desire to provide explanatory models in evidence here, as children try to actively use their limited knowledge about second-hand goods, consumers seeking out lower prices, and the competition that follows between retailers. It is certainly not evidence of guesswork, perversity or ignorance.

We should be equally sceptical of suggestions that many young children seem to be unaware of the origin of familiar products. Firstly, children will often answer questions with a high degree of literalism; just as money 'comes from' shops, so does milk 'come from' a shop. They may also be aware (perhaps from television) that milk is bottled or put in cartons on a production line, so the answer that milk 'comes from a machine' also has a certain truth to it. The knowledge that some goods are manufactured may be extended to cover natural products, which are often as uniform in appearance as though they had come from a factory. The children then 'invent' a process to explain how the product was manufactured. Hutchings (1989: 13) describes examples of these accounts: 'bananas come on trees, then they go to the factory to be put in skins' (4 year-old); 'oranges – they make it all out of juice – the juice what you make – they pour it all in the sink and they make the skin of it and then they put it on' (6 year-old).

That there are differences in economic understanding between children in different social classes, as is suggested by Tizard and Hughes and others cited above indicates that the development of economic understanding is unlikely to be linked simply to a maturational process. Working-class children are better at understanding the nature of money and work, and the relationship between the two. This is because it is a more central aspect of their domestic experiences. Further evidence of this is provided from cross-cultural studies.

Jahoda (1981) studied Scottish children's understanding of the economic functions of banks and shops. He found that while his subjects, aged 12 to 16, understood the concept of profit in a shop (of which they had some direct experience), they had difficulty transferring this understanding to banking. But when the experiment was replicated by Jahoda (1983) with younger children whose mothers largely worked as traders in street markets, he found that these children achieved an understanding of profit at a much earlier age. Extending the study to Dutch children, he found that twice as many of the older Dutch children realized that money could be borrowed from a bank, compared to the Scottish children.

Studies by Hong Kwang and Stacey (1977) comparing children in Australia and Hong Kong, suggest that while the Hong Kong children's ideas developed in approximately the same order as the Australian group, they achieved a level of sophistication at much younger ages: profit was understood at 6, and the workings of a bank at 10.

The social and economic experiences of a child thus have an important bearing on his or her capacity to understand and handle a particular concept. However, the experience in itself is likely not to be sufficient. The examples from Hutchings quoted above show children struggling to impose some logic and order on their experiential observations, not always with success. Developing ideas originally expressed by Vygotsky (1962), Barbara Rogoff (1986: 38) suggests that socialization is a joint process, in which children and adults interact: 'together, children and adults choose learning situations and calibrate the child's level of participation so that the child is comfortably challenged'. Children do not 'passively observe adults and extract the information spontaneously . . . the child . . . adjusts the [adult's] pace of instruction and guides the adult in constructing the scaffold' (ibid.: 81).

Such a pattern of learning requires the participation of adults, but David Wood (1986: 210) has pointed to the difficulties teachers have, in school situations, in effectively responding to such prompts from the child. In practice 'it is the child who must make his or her thinking contingent upon that of the teacher. If children are able and willing to be contingent upon the thought processes and actions of another, then learning may proceed. If they are not, then it seems unlikely that learning will follow'. For Wood, this suggested failure or lack of progress by a learner is attributable 'not simply to factors located "in" the child but to constraints that arise as an emergent property of teacher–learner interactions [which are] in turn tightly constrained by the nature of the institutions that we have invented to bring teachers and learners together' (Wood 1986: 210). To this must be added, in the case of the economic learning considered in this chapter, the child's and the adult's own experiences of the social and economic environment.

It has been shown that it is possible for young children to understand and use economic and industrial ideas, provided that they have had both a variety of experiences and the opportunity to construct these in a social setting with more experienced practitioners. However, it has been argued that to allow children to develop, albeit imperfectly, explanations of the current system, is to passively reinforce existing stereotypes and patterns of behaviour. Clearly, capitalism ought to be able to justify itself on grounds of argument and logic, and not simply rely on an unquestioning acceptance of the *status quo*. If we do not encourage a critical awareness of economic relationships in young people, they will grow up assuming that the system that we have is simply the natural order of things.

The evidence suggests that when given the opportunity to assess and evaluate social and economic activity, children prove to be remarkably persistent in making naïve moral judgements about the fairness or otherwise of adult relationships. By naïve, I mean innocent and candid, rather than immature. The sections that follow will give many examples of this concern with fairness: in hierarchical relationships and gender relationships at work, and in the distribution of profits, power and authority. There are also examples of the preceding point: of acceptance of existing practices as inevitable. The argument for education for economic and industrial awareness must ultimately be not just that children can intellectually cope with the issues (given the experience and the scaffolding referred to), nor that it is socially or economically necessary that they do so, but that it is essential that future citizens have a critical understanding of systems, and are capable of making informed decisions about the continuity or change of such systems.

What should the current agenda be for economic and industrial understanding?

The consumerist society that has become a feature of capitalist society in the developed first world countries necessitates a more consumer-aware and critical reaction from the public, while the development of what has sometimes been described as a post-industrial society requires future citizens to have a much broader view of the place of work and leisure in society.

Property

One of the most fundamental ideas in the development of economies has been that of property. Since the 17th century, the notion of the individual possessing property rights has been part of the Western European tradition on which modern capitalism has been based. Ownership and rights over property became commodified and transferable, replacing the pre-modern forms of the concepts: 'the basic assumption of possessive individualism [is] that man is free and human by virtue of his sole proprietorship of his own person, and that human society is essentially a series of market relationships' (Macpherson 1962: 270). Possessive individualism made it become possible to trade in land and other means of production, enhancing the unequal distribution of property, and breaking the usufructuary relationship between the user and the land that existed for the majority of the population. The establishment of transferable property rights was a crucial element in the creation of a landless class, that had to trade its labour – its only asset – in order to survive. Given that this idea of property underlies the entire economic structure of the country, it is remarkable that it does not appear at all within CG4.

Why is this so? It can hardly be a desire to keep hidden the nature of capitalism, because the overwhelming tenor of the document is capitalistic. To be sure, there is the occasional reference to a plurality of economic systems, but the dominant economic philosophy put forward by the National Curriculum Council is neo-liberal and market-dominated, and ownership is a crucial element of this. Perhaps it is no more than an oversight (Ahier 1992).

The role envisaged for education in CG4 seems to be largely one of cultural transmission. It seems deeply embedded in the idea that if only the schools could inculcate children into a positive attitude towards entrepreneurial activity and the necessity for 'sound economic stewardship' (that is, monetarism), then all would be well for the nation's prosperity.

Surplus

Industrial production techniques have, since the early 1950s, been more than adequate to produce sufficient basic needs and requirements for all our citizens (even though the distributive systems of the state may not allow all citizens adequate access to them). Industry now is largely concerned with producing additional goods and services, marginal to basic needs, and the only way in which it can sell these goods and services is to persuade consumers that they need these items. Advertising and marketing create a market that did not previously exist. Moreover, the durability and reliability of many manufactured items is now very good, so much so that they do not need replacing regularly – or at least, not sufficiently frequently to allow industries to continue to produce the goods at the same or greater levels. The solution that has been adopted is to create styles and fashions that require goods to be discarded and rejected before they are fully used – perceptions of goods and services are manipulated to that they are perceived of as obsolescent before they wear out, and are therefore replaced while still usable. In many instances, the power of the producer (and their advertisers) has become so marked that it has been necessary for the state to intervene to control the most blatant excesses.

Employment

Linked to these have been major structural changes in employment. Fewer people are now engaged in manufacture. The proportion of home workers, part-time work, and the like has grown. Skills become redundant, and even newly-developed and acquired skills become obsolescent. Fewer individuals are in employment, and thus each employed individual has to support the needs of more non-employed individuals, either through the family economy or through the state economy. Yet the needs of the economy as a whole require more individuals to be engaged in consumption, particularly of goods that are essentially peripheral to needs and the development of an underclass of people with low incomes undermines this – and has potential implications for political stability.

These are the economic issues that are important today, and yet they find no place in either the monetarist economics of the state, nor a place in the nostrums of CG4. But, as the next section will argue, these are issues that are within the domain of children's understanding, and which many of them would see as important.

What does this mean in terms of children's understanding and of the primary school curriculum?

Many young children are aware that they are part of a consumer culture. Advertisements are certainly designed to encourage them to either be consumers, or to exert pressure on parents and guardians to act as consumers on their behalf. But many children have also developed critical approaches to advertisements. Children analyse advertisements, and in particular many seem able to deconstruct the images and the texts of television advertisements. Many children as young as 7 or 8 are aware of and can describe the advertisers' ploys, and are fully aware of their intentions. They also parody advertisers' jingles in playground rhymes: the following examples were picked up in a north London primary school:

My Little Pony,
All Skinny and Boney

GI Joe, International Zeros
[originally: 'International Heroes']

Masked Crusaders
The stupid ones
With the big fat bums
[of Mask toys]

A Mars a Day
Helps your teeth rot away
[originally: 'Helps you work, rest and play']

The first three rhymes are based on advertisements for themed collectable toys, heavily marketed on television, and of American origin. The children's jingles deliberately reverse the image that the original advertisement was intended to convey: My Little Pony toys are a range of soft plastic ponies, with plump bodies and groomable manes and tails; GI Joe are a series of action dolls with movable posable limbs, each with particular accessories (weapons, defensive equipment, etc.), a name and biography, while Mask toys are fantasy military-style vehicles peopled by the 'masked crusaders'. The final rhyme is for a sweet marketed for its nutritional powers; again, the children's version turns the meaning back on the original.

Young children also develop an awareness of capitalism: many of them realize that money is a commodity that has a price, and that it can be necessary to borrow it in order to start a venture. The following example is of a girl, Kelly, aged 11 years 5 months, in an inner London primary school (Ross 1989, see also Ross 1992: 112):

Interviewer: Where else can you go besides a bank to borrow money?
Kelly: Er, money-lenders, but they're cons . . . they're money sharks, they say that they want more money than the bank, don't they? They charge extra.
Interviewer: Does the bank charge extra?
Kelly: Dunno, probably, but the money sharks do more . . . If they didn't have the money in the bank, they wouldn't get a profit from it. The bank wouldn't get the profit. Say you had a building society, your money in it, you get some money on it, some extra money. Because they

use your money, and they get extra money, they give the
extra bit back, like fifty-fifty back, like in a reward.

This is not simply a passive acceptance of the known world, as it is (though
it is also this). When asked at first about the distribution of profits, for
example, she treats the question descriptively: this is what happens, and,
as far as she is concerned at this level, this is a sufficient explanation. Asked
why the manager or owner should get paid most, she replied:

Kelly: Cos it's his! The profit goes to him. When all the bills
and stuff are paid then the profit out of that goes to
him.
Interviewer: Is that fair?
Kelly: Well, it's the way it goes, innit?

Pushed a little further, she shows an ability to actively construct an argument to support her observations of the *status quo*. She puts forward two
justifications, one based on equity for the risk-taker, and the other prag-
matic, both showing an acute awareness of the perspectives and motivations
of entrepreneurs and employees.

Interviewer: I didn't say 'is that the way it is?', I said 'is it fair?'
Kelly: Yes, well, it *is* fair. Because these people [indicating picture of workforce] are working hard, and he can't run
it . . .
Interviewer: But if they're working hard, shouldn't they have the
profits?
Kelly: No, they get their money, they get paid, but they don't
get the profit, they're just getting paid for what they're
doing. Which is just that, their job. And the rest goes
to him. Cos otherwise, if he didn't get any money out
of that, no one would set any business up, would they?
. . . Cos they'd think. 'What's the point of going into
there if you don't get nothing?'

Much of the work that has been done with primary-aged children in this
area has focused on activities in which children plan manufacturing
activities, or service activities, and then market and sell them. This conception of the mini-enterprise in the primary school classroom was developed
first in the United States as the kinder-economy (Kourilsky 1977, 1983),
and developed in Britain (for example Williams *et al.* 1984; Smith 1988).
It might also be noted that there have been some serious criticisms about
the way in which such activities have concentrated almost exclusively on
the mechanics of production, to the exclusion of any development of economic ideas (HMI 1990).

Wealth creation in practice is rather more complex than this reductionist approach might suggest. The underlying philosophy of the mini-enterprise strategy is to demonstrate that goods and services have an origin, and that people cooperatively use a range of skills to provide and market them. The following classroom discussion began with a discussion on the Roman economy in Britain. The teacher is trying to use an import–export model to demonstrate the balance of trade, and asks the children to transfer the argument to a contemporary British context. (Susan is 9 years 9 months, Nicola 9 years 11 months and Leslie 10 years 6 months):

> *Teacher:* ... do you think we'd get richer if we sold more things to other countries or if we buy more from other countries?
> *Susan, Nicola, Leslie (simultaneously):* Sold.
> *Nicola:* Because if you buy things, you're not going to get rich.
> *Susan:* No, but if you sell them and buy them and you buy them you'd be selling them, and then you'd get rich.
> *Teacher:* But why not just sell them first?
> *Susan:* But you wouldn't have them. You've got to buy them to get them, haven't you?
>
> (Ross 1993)

Susan's perception of how to become wealthy is rather different from her teacher's model. The teacher is first creating a category (of the country, identified as 'we', as opposed to 'other countries'), and second putting forward a simple balance of trade model in which 'we' sell 'them' what we have, and they sell us what they have. Susan's reaction to the categorization is unclear, although it could be argued that her use of 'you' shows that she was assuming that individuals were involved, not the generalized categories constructed by her teacher. But she clearly believes that trading involves both buying and selling, not just producing and selling: 'you've got to buy them to get them'.

Another group of children in the same class showed an understanding of the tendency towards consumerism (see the section on 'Surplus', above). Michael is 10 years 6 months:

> *Michael:* Well, another thing, if we, we don't really need, we've already got loads of video-cameras and videos, we don't really need more really. So why are we importing, we're always importing things ...
>
> (Ross 1993)

Michael's argument is that it is possible to go beyond satisfying needs and wants; this is picked up later in the same conversation by Katriona (10 years 1 month), who identifies other limiting factors on the growth in production:

Katriona: If you made everything in this country, then the country
would be full of fact—, full of factories and things like
that, and that's why not everything should be made in this
country ...

(Ross 1993)

Children also think about unemployment, and the consequences of this.
This 10 year-old boy in a south London school accurately identifies the
scale of the problem, the causes of it, his source of information, and adds
a prediction:

Ian: There's so many factories – like all last week I heard on the news
that there was three factories closing down in one week alone,
and there's about three million people out of work now. They're
just going to close down factories and keep it like that.

(Ross 1983: 17)

The possible changes in employment structure are equally clear to some
children. In particular, many girls are aware of changes in gender roles, and
the implications that these might have for them. Jane is in the same school
as Ian, and is also 10. She uses the experiences of her neighbours, and
transfers it smoothly to a projection of her own life, but does this in the
context of a wide-ranging class discussion on women's possibilities in
employment:

Jane: My next door neighbour, they were both teachers, but the
man stopped being a teacher and so the woman went to
work and the man stayed at home.
Teacher: And did you think that was OK?
Jane: Yes, he got on very well. I'd really like it if I was his wife,
having a nice meal cooked for me when I got home. He
done all the cleaning, looked after the baby ...

(Ross 1983: 17)

Changes in employment are also predicted by children in the growing
automation that they perceive, both in the home and in the workplace. The
following conversation was recorded at the time when microwave ovens
were first making an impact on the domestic market:

Marion: Barry said [. . .] that ladies have always been in the kitchen.
I don't see why, 'cos I think that in the future, when there's
all special machines like microwave cookers, I didn't think
they're going to be in the kitchen all the time, I think they
ought to go out and work. In the future, nearly every house
will have one, so they just have to pop it in ... and they
won't have to spend all their time cooking.

Teacher: Right anyone . . . well, it's Barry, it's his point to come back on, Barry . . .

Barry: In the future they'll have all these machines – if they have so many machines, why work?

(Ross 1983: 18)

Automation and the leisure society is also perceived as a possibility. Joe (aged 10) places this in the future, but not in his own personal future:

Joe: In 5000 AD they won't need no cooks and nothing like that – they might have robots, and like that . . . it's like Unipart, they don't have to employ workers any more, they've got robots to make the parts.

(Ross 1983: 18)

The curricular implications of these examples of children's interpretations of their current economic surroundings are to suggest that children's abilities are underestimated. They are underestimated by the authors of CG4, whose suggestions are skewed towards the neo-liberal emphasis on the market as the sole determinant of value, and who apparently imagine that children will accept the somewhat blue-tinted vision of the world which that document portrays. They are also underestimated by many teachers, who find it difficult (for many and often understandable reasons) to use children's own experiences and attempted explanations of the economic world, and to harness this to children's naïve sense of fairness.

The curriculum in primary schools *might* offer room for these ideas to be developed. An alternative – or even simply an additional – set of concepts might provide a focus: property and ownership, division of profits, gender roles at work, hierarchical relationships in power and authority, unemployment and leisure. Such an agenda would need to be related to children's own pre-existing experiences, and to those experiences offered to children through the school, such as visits to workplaces in which children get a chance to talk with other adults. One of the fundamental difficulties with CG4, and the ideology that created it, is that it is based on the belief that children need an explanation of the 'economic realities'. While it is possible to object to the particular 'realities' as partisan, the educator's more fundamental rejection must be on the grounds that it is for children themselves to construct and test explanations.

Teachers need, therefore, to develop a critical stance as they develop work in the areas described in CG4. But this should not act as a limitation on the range of learning activities they provide. There are three basic sets of experientially based activities that seem to be most fruitful in developing acute attitudes.

Developing a series of visits with a local workplace can be one of the most fruitful ways of working. Ideally, this would be a continuing relationship over several weeks, involving both children repeatedly visiting a workplace, and members of the workplace visiting the school, and involve a workplace that does something rather different from places that they may already have experienced (whether directly or indirectly). A number of pointers emerge from many of the case studies of such visits. First, try to focus the children's attentions on those at work, rather than on the technicalities of the processes involved. Children will learn more generalizable knowledge from investigating the hierarchy of a factory than they will from studying the conveyor belt system! This will involve the children talking to as wide a range of people as possible, ascertaining their views and experiences (and not relying simply on the PR-patter of the personnel officer who shows the children around). Second, children should be encouraged to discuss their expectations of what they will find before they go: the learning that will arise from the juxtaposition of their (possibly unrealistic) expectations from the reality of the experience will be greater if they have formally articulated their preconceptions. Third, they should discuss with the teacher the experiences after the event, the teacher if necessary drawing their attention to some of the contentious issues that may have been encountered. Visits made by members of the workforce back to the school can be used to check additional requests for information, for interviews, or for participating in role plays.

A second group of activities concern mini-enterprises. In these, a group of children or a class become involved in identifying a need, planning to meet it, and then carrying out the enterprise necessary to deliver it. Many mini-enterprises involve providing goods or services, but they could equally include the planning and provision of a charitable activity (such as a tea-party for elderly people). Identification of needs and requirements, developing personal skills, planning and the management of funds are all important aspects of a mini-enterprise. It can be very easy for the activity to be diverted into a craft/technology exercise, with more emphasis on the making and less on the economic/social implications. Again, therefore, discussion and debriefing will form an important part of the teaching agenda, so that children can identify and conceptualize the more essential learning areas.

Finally, role-play and simulations allow enactive learning, in which children can use their experiences to support roles of people at work, and the difficulties and opportunities that arise. For example, a class of children could be divided into those making models or Christmas decorations individually, and those working on a production line. The discussion that follows could usefully compare their experiences – of the number of items made, their quality, of the children's ability to socialize as they worked, and so on.

The key feature in all three sets of activities lies in the discussion that surrounds them. The value of experiential learning lies largely in this inter-change of ideas, rather than simply in the experience *per se*.

There are many other resources available, but most published materials need to be approached with deliberate caution. Firms and organizations supplying teaching materials often produce materials that, despite their fine design features, colour and quality of production, have serious problems with their learning aims and strategies. As a rule of thumb, the somewhat less prepossessing materials produced by Development Education centres, trade unions and cooperatives will have much greater learning potential, and develop a more critical awareness, than the public relations approach of most industries.

Conclusion

CG4 claims a spurious objectivity and authenticity, and projects an explanatory framework that is both rigid and partial. This itself is of great concern, and not only because it might alienate teachers. More fundamentally, it leaves little room for children to address issues that arise out of any but the most transient 'workplace visit' experience.

There are other needs that children have that should be addressed. Children need to be helped to construct explanatory models that relate to their own and their families' experiences of the economic. In particular, they could be encouraged to bring their sense of fairness to such issues as:

- the distribution of the ownership of property of all kinds;
- the distribution of power and authority within an economic unit;
- consumerism: the manufacture of commodities that can then only be sold through the manipulative creation of needs and desires through advertising;
- consumption: the unnecessary uses of finite resources;
- the possibilities and implications of a proportion of the population not being in paid employment;
- the relative distribution of wealth between different parts of the world, as well as within each part.

All of these issues are economic, but they hardly figure in CG4. They are all questions that will be have to be considered in the near future.

References

Ahier, J. (1988) *Industry, Children and the Nation: An Analysis of National Identity in School Textbooks*. Lewes: Falmer.

Ahier, J. (1992) Economics for children in the United States and Britain, in M. Hutchings and W. Wade (eds) *Developing Economic and Industrial Understanding in the Primary School*. London: PNL Press.

Campbell, R. (1986) quoted at a National Association for Pastoral Care in Education conference, *Times Educational Supplement*, 12 December.

Carrington, B. and Troyna, B. (eds) (1988) *Children and Controversial Issues: Strategies for the Early and Middle Years of Schooling*. Lewes: Falmer Press.

Dunn, J. (1988) *The Beginnings of Social Understanding*. Oxford: Blackwell.

Graham, D. (with Tytler, D.) (1993) *A Lesson for Us All: The Making of the National Curriculum*. London: Routledge.

Harber, C. (1980) Teaching the politics of everyday life. *Social Science Teacher*, 10(2): a supplement I–IV.

HMI (1990) *Mini-enterprise in Schools: Some Aspects of Current Practice*. London: DES.

Holt, J. (1984) *How Children Fail*. Harmondsworth: Penguin.

Hong Kwang, R. and Stacey, B. (1977) The understanding of socio-economic concepts in Malaysian Chinese school children. *Child Study Journal*, 11: 33–49.

Hutchings, M. (1989) Children's ideas about the world of work, in A. Ross, M. Hutchings and A. Craft (eds) *The Primary Enterprise Pack*. London: PNL Press.

Hutchings, M. (1993) Talking about adult work with young children. *Early Child Development and Care*, 94: 51–65.

Jahoda, G. (1981) The development of thinking about economic institutions: the bank. *Cahiers de Psychologie Cognitive*, 1(1): 55–78.

Jahoda, G. (1983) European 'lag' in the development of an economic concept: a study in Zimbabwe. *British Journal of Developmental Psychology*, 1: 110–23.

Kourilsky, M. (1977) The kinder-economy: a case study of kindergarten pupil's acquisition of economic concepts. *The Elementary School Journal*, 77(3), January: 182–91.

Kourilsky, M. (1983) *Mini-Society: Experiencing real-world economics in the elementary school classroom*. Menlo Park, Ca: Addison Wesley.

McNaughton, A. (1966) Piaget's theory and primary school social science. *Educational Review*, 19 November: 23–32.

Macpherson, C. (1962) *The Political Theory of Possessive Individualism*. Oxford: Oxford University Press.

Maital, S. (1982) *Minds, Markets and Money*. New York: Basic Books.

National Curriculum Council (NCC) (1990) *Curriculum Guidance 4: Education for Economic and Industrial Understanding*. York: NCC.

Piaget, J. (1965) *The Child's Conception of the World*. St Albans: Paladin.

Rogoff, B. (1986) Adult assistance of children's learning, in T. Raphael (ed.) *The Contexts of School Based Literacy*. New York: Random House.

Ross, A. (1983) The bottle stopper factory: talking all together. *The English Magazine*, 11: 14–18.

Ross, A. (1989) Research data gathered in an inner London school (unpublished).

Ross, A. (1992) Children's perceptions of capital, in M. Hutchings and W. Wade (eds) *Developing Economic and Industrial Understanding in the Primary School*. London: PNL Press.

Ross, A. (1993) Terms of trade: children's discussion about trading. Paper presented to the *Third Research Conference on the Economic and Industrial Understanding of Children up to the Age of Eleven*, University of North London, September 1993.

Smith, D. (1988) *Industry in the Primary School Curriculum: Principles and Practice*. Lewes: Falmer.

Thomas, N. (1993) Breadth, balance and the National Curriculum, in J. Campbell (ed.) *Breadth and Balance in the Primary Curriculum*. London: Falmer.

Tizard, B. and Hughes, M. (1984) *Young Children Learning: Talking and thinking at Home and at School*. London: Fontana.

Vygotsky, J. (1962) *Thought and Language*. Cambridge, MA: MIT Press.

Walkerdine, V. (1988) *The Mastery of Reason: Cognitive Development and the Production of Rationality*. London: Routledge.

Walkerdine, V. and Lucey, H. (1989) *Democracy in the Kitchen: The Regulation of Mothers and the Socialisation of Daughters*. London: Virago.

Wiener, M. (1981) *English Culture and the Decline of the Industrial Spirit, 1850–1980*. Cambridge: Cambridge University Press.

Williams, J., Revill, C. and Garem Jones, R. (1984) The schools–industry primary project, Clwyd, in I. Jamieson (ed.) *'We Make Kettles': Studying Industry in the Primary School*. York: Longman.

Wood, D. (1986) Aspects of teaching and learning, in M. Richards and P. Light (eds) *Children of Social Worlds*. Cambridge: Polity Press.

7

VAL MILLMAN

Catching them young: careers education in the primary school

If only I had known then what I know now.

Editors' introduction

Val Millman's chapter is concerned with another set of issues
related to economic and industrial understanding. In
common with Alistair Ross, Val Millman identifies a number
of areas that need to be developed beyond the curriculum
guidance currently offered. Val discusses the implications of
employment trends to educational provision. The realities of
structural unemployment, de-skilling and increased part-time
and temporary employment are considered along with
changing gender roles and the implications of enduring
racism and sexism.

Val reviews current careers educational provision and
offers examples of a number of valuable classroom
approaches. She provides a vision of a school where children
may learn about careers through experiencing many of the
related practices and procedures. They may advertise for
classroom jobs to be filled by 'monitors', apply for the post
of 'part-time school telephone operator' or 'visitors' guide'.
Training and re-training issues associated with such tasks
may also be dealt with by children actively involved in the
organization of their school. She also suggests a range of
other strategies involving role-play and simulation.

As Val argues, children may usefully discuss the various
jobs that they do at home; how the labour is divided within

the family, the classroom and the school. Their pocket money may or may not be considered as wages by parents, and children may meaningfully consider issues of incentives and collective bargaining in these contexts.

Introduction

As adults, when we look back at the pattern of our lives we can identify influences and turning points that have led us to where we are now. We can reflect on the opportunities that life has presented us with from a young age and the ways we have reacted to those opportunities or sought them out when they were not readily available to us. We can analyse the part that circumstances played in shaping our decisions; if only we had known then what we know now ...

My own 'career path' has been the product of a variety of influences and circumstances, from within and beyond school. What appears on paper to have been a relatively smooth and linear process has, in fact, evolved as a result of sometimes arbitrary and haphazard responses to life events. Our lives and our possibilities do not fit easily into self-contained compartments any more than our learning fits neatly into discretely packaged areas of the curriculum. Careers education is as much about understanding and gaining control over the ways in which the bits of our lives can be pieced together as it is about identifying when, how and which part of the labour market we may participate in as adults. Careers education is therefore about far more than qualifications and aspirations. It is about knowledge and understanding of our world and our place within it, our attitudes, relationships, skills and expectations. In schools this learning takes place throughout the curriculum – and it is these aspects of learning that have traditionally formed the most important foundations of the primary school curriculum.

In this chapter I shall first establish the form and extent of careers education that currently takes place within the school curriculum. I shall underline the importance of continuity in this area of the curriculum across all key stages of compulsory schooling and briefly outline the areas of evidence that schools will be required to demonstrate when they are inspected under the Office for Standards in Education (OFSTED) criteria for the inspection of pupil welfare and guidance. All schools, including primaries, are required to provide a curriculum which prepares pupils for adult life; this chapter will consider what the future holds for our current primary school children and will urge teachers to equip children to succeed in 'the reality of the world of work rather than with some illusion of what it should be like' (Watts 1993).

The second half of the chapter will consider how the essential elements of careers education can be built into the primary school curriculum. Examples of different approaches will be described which either have careers education objectives as their major focus or constitute a context for learning in which relevant concepts and skills can be incidentally developed. Each of these approaches are valid components of a school's careers education programme and need to be planned and evaluated in the context of curriculum policies and schemes of work.

Early foundations of careers education: in the home corner

Let's first look at an example of how some of the foundations of careers education are already in place in the early years curriculum. Consider the reception class teacher who became concerned at the repetitiveness of children's play within the home corner of her classroom and concerned at the limitations this was putting on their learning. This teacher decided to use the home corner to create a range of fantasy worlds through which children would broaden their perceptions of their own roles as well as the roles of others.

In the home corner she had observed that the girls were continually cleaning, cooking and looking after numerous babies while the boys frequently disrupted this by being 'bad dogs', 'painters and decorators' and 'robbers'. She speculated that the boys' behaviour might result from feeling that the girls had control over the major home roles. She hoped that the introduction of fantasy worlds beyond the home might give boys more scope for imaginative play and encourage girls to rehearse a wider range of roles. Her discussions with pupils resulted in the home corner becoming a café, complete with cooks, waiters and waitresses and customers. She said:

> The children were very enthusiastic about the home corner's conversion and despite the fact that it was, on a few occasions overrun by 'big, bad, dogs', visited by painters and decorators and burgled, the role play was most successful ... At later dates the home corner also became a medical centre with nurses, patients, doctors and administrative support.
>
> The girls found it much easier to take on the new roles than the boys. The girls were better organized and more imaginative but interestingly the boys did begin to take on the more caring roles within the centre. Likewise when the corner was a railway station, boys adopted creative roles that contained certain built-in constraints on their behaviour. Sometimes when in the role of drivers they found themselves having to wait patiently as passengers waiting their turn,

and as guards having to wait until everything was ready before blowing the whistle.

(Millman and Shipton 1994: 159)

The home corner is an area of the classroom where the focus of children's play is most often on adult roles in the home and on the relationship of these roles to activities outside the home. Interestingly it is also often an area of learning in which adults in the classroom make minimum intervention despite evidence, that we shall later explore, that adults have an important role in structuring these activities. The example above demonstrates that careers education is indeed taking place within the early years curriculum of schools, albeit not explicitly 'timetabled'. Within the home corner children are exploring and rehearsing roles and relationships, developing attitudes and skills and shaping expectations and aspirations for their futures.

In the above example, as a result of observation and review, the teacher decided to make changes in this aspect of the curriculum. She identified a range of specific learning objectives for particular groups of children. Both girls and boys needed new and non-stereotypical opportunities for role-play; the boys needed to develop restraint and learn to take turns; the girls needed to learn to share space they had got used to making their own. Together with the children the teacher devised activities through which these objectives could be achieved without losing the fun and spontaneity that had previously been enjoyed. This teacher was building careers education into her early years curriculum; by using a planned and interventionist approach she intended to ensure that all children were participating in experiences that would give them the skills, self-confidence and perceptions to gain access to a wider range of roles.

How much careers education is already taking place in schools?

The Education Reform Act (DES 1988) promised to give careers education a high priority in the curriculum careers education and guidance a high priority in the curriculum seeing it as is an integral part of the preparation of pupils for the opportunities, responsibilities and experiences of adult life. The National Curriculum Council (NCC) identified careers education as one of the five cross-curricular themes. The five associated 'grey booklets' of Curriculum Guidance (National Curriculum Council 1990) were published to provide primary and secondary schools with appropriate guidance on management strategies and approaches to content delivery of the five cross-curricular themes. But the guidance booklets did not have the status or force of the statutory subject orders and most have remained unread on the headteacher's 'pending' shelf. In practice the rapid and ill-thought through introduction of an overcrowded National Curriculum resulted in careers education being progressively squeezed out of the primary curriculum.

In contrast to the impact of the National Curriculum, The Technical and Vocational Educational Initiative (TVEI) had earlier stimulated increased activity in secondary schools at the education-industry interface. This was also an increasing trend in some primary schools, especially where business representatives on governing bodies were beginning to take a more active role in school life. Sadly though, many schools which put energy into establishing innovative 'education–industry' programmes, including out-of-school visits and visiting speakers, often did not build these activities into their curriculum plans in ways which ensured coherence and continuity of learning for pupils. For many pupils these have remained 'one-off' activities rather than ones from which broader lessons could be learned. Experience shows that there is as great a need for careful key stage planning in cross-curricular areas as there is within the subject curriculum. More so where the school chooses to deliver careers education and education for industrial understanding through the subject curriculum rather than through designated space on the timetable. It is possible that the timetabled time which the Dearing review of the National Curriculum Orders (Dearing 1994), promised to 'free up' will result in an increased ability and determination of schools to plan careers education into the curriculum from early in Key Stage One.

At the same time as Sir Ron Dearing was undertaking the review of the National Curriculum, the government published a White Paper, *Competitiveness* (DoE 1994a) which announced that almost 90 million pounds would be invested in careers education and guidance over the next three years. This investment of resources, albeit with its major emphasis on secondary schools, is likely to mean that there will be close scrutiny of this area of the curriculum in future. The OFSTED *Handbook for the Inspection of Schools* (1994) underlines the place of careers education in the whole curriculum. It has a clear expectation that such issues will be addressed in primary as well as in secondary schools. In Part 2, Section 7.7 of the OFSTED (1994) handbook referring to Pupils' Welfare and Guidance, the evaluation criteria are as follows: The quality of welfare and guidance is to be evaluated by judging the effectiveness with which the school discharges its duty of care for pupils, including: 'measures taken by the school to identify and meet pupils' academic and personal needs and to provide curricular and careers guidance' (OFSTED 1994, 7.7: 34). The Inspection Framework acknowledges that evidence of the school's guidance programme may be dispersed across a number of subject areas, including personal and social education. Although some of the areas of evidence identified in the Framework are clearly more pertinent to secondary than to primary schools the following examples of inspection evidence could be examined in either:

- Pupils' attitudes to people, property, work, school and the community and the environment;
- Positive and effective links with industry and the wider community;
- A school curriculum which prepares pupils for adult life; whole curriculum planning and coherent provision for cross-curricular issues.

Schools are now having to place increased emphasis on continuity across key stages and on pupils receiving appropriate guidance at key points of transition. The smooth transfer and sensible use of pupil records at times of transition is an essential basis for the successful personal, educational and career development of the child. It is essential for pupils that primary schools interpret careers education curriculum aims in a consistent and coherent manner, and vital that teachers have a view of the adult world for which they are preparing their pupils that is up to date, well-founded and securely grounded in the school's policies and ethos.

A school curriculum which prepares pupils for adult life

For most primary school teachers there appear to be more immediate educational aims and objectives than preparation of their pupils for adult life in general and the world of work in particular. But recent government interventions such as the introduction of the National Curriculum have reminded us of the dynamic relationship between educational processes, institutions and the curriculum, and wider changes in the social, economic and cultural fabric of society. There is no doubt that both primary and secondary schooling are seen to play a major role in preparing young people to meet the future needs of the adult labour market. Most schools' curriculum policies identify teaching and learning strategies that aim to maximize the potential of *all* children; these strategies assume an active role for the growing child in shaping her or his future and in developing a range of positive responses to the constraints and opportunities that the adult world will present.

Although the relationship of present learning to future role is rarely explicit in the day-to-day context of young children, the ways in which we organize our teaching are indeed based on assumptions about our pupils' future, as too are the standards we set for them and the expectations we have of them. If we are serious about our commitment to their individual entitlement and the realization of their individual potential we have to be sure that our aims and objectives will equip them to find a route through their future lives which can include their participation in the world of work. We need to think carefully about how we should prepare them to maximize their life chances, and this thinking must be based on a well-informed view of how their future may be different from our present.

Beyond 2000

Beyond the year 2000 it seems likely that people's working lives will become increasingly discontinuous and fragmented, including periods of unemployment, education and training, and part- and full-time work. At present, it is unclear whether it is the short-term effects of the recent recession or more profound structural changes that we are seeing in the labour market, for example: more prolonged periods of high unemployment, heightened job insecurity, increases in part-time work. The government strategy to make Britain more competitive in the world markets is to boost our overall skill level and increase post-16 participation in education and training. Employers are seeking to create an increasingly flexible workforce in terms both of patterns of work and training and of the pool of workers available to them as the composition of the adult workforce gets older – the capacity to employ the elderly or those with disabilities for example. 10 per cent of employers are now offering home-based work, 5 per cent telebased work, part-time employment now constitutes 24 per cent of all employment and 46 per cent of female employment (DoE 1994b). Full-time work is increasingly subject to short-term contracts, and by the year 2000 the self-employed are likely to constitute 13 per cent of the workforce in this country.

The labour market is currently segmented both by sex and by skill level. Most growth in the foreseeable future will be in the service sector, a traditionally female area of work, and in higher level jobs with many traditional areas of male employment disappearing; in manufacturing for example. In the future, many men are likely to have to accept periods of unemployment or lower wage part-time work.

While some sections of the black community have now reached the same levels in the workplace as their counterparts (Jones 1993) they still face barriers of racism and discrimination and areas of work that are difficult to access. African Caribbean, Pakistani and Bengali men are more likely to be unemployed.

Although women over the next decade are likely to account for almost half the workforce, at present 46 per cent of female employment is in part-time low-wage jobs with poor job security and working conditions. The average hourly wage of women is only 78 per cent of men's. In 1989 women were only 27 per cent of those employed in management positions.

The picture therefore is one of uncertainty and discontinuity in employment for most sections of the population with some groups likely to face more barriers than others in access to well-paid continuous employment and in access to support structures in times of hardship. As other contributors to this book argue, these are inequalities that schools can and should contribute to redressing and eliminating. Alongside this is the probability that individuals will be part of a variety of family structures at different times in their adult lives; roles and responsibilities in the home will need to be as flexible as roles and responsibilities in the workplace. Employers will need to create ways of facilitating smooth transitions between the two and will have to manage the effects of these transitions. Both women and men will have to develop a bank of transferable skills as well as the mental, emotional and physical capacity to move between roles. They will need to build an identity that is broadly based, capable of responding to change but also strong enough to manage and maintain some control over change; to challenge and negotiate the basis on which changes take place whether in the home or in the workplace. Skills and qualifications will continue to determine individual access to educational, training and employment opportunities from an early age and throughout life.

Key elements of careers education in the primary school

In this context it seems unarguable that key elements of careers education should be built into the primary curriculum – indeed, many of them are already there. What may be more contentious is to what extent it seems helpful, or indeed necessary, to label these aspects of the curriculum as 'careers educational' or its equivalent. Why not just leave things as they are?

Our experience of curriculum overload and competing pressures for time in recent years is that those areas outside statutory orders have, despite good intentions, been squeezed off the curriculum agenda of our classrooms. Some teachers have managed to hang on to 'important bits' of the non-statutory curriculum but the teaching of these 'bits' has often not offered much coherence to the pupils. A planned approach to the inclusion of careers education in the curriculum, although not necessarily as a distinct area, offers a number of advantages. First, it is a means of defending its curriculum space from encroachment by other subjects. Second, it ensures that pupils are prepared for this aspect of the secondary curriculum during Key Stages One and Two in as coherent and purposeful a manner as they will be prepared for other subjects. Third, it facilitates a consistent approach across the school which can be readily demonstrated to parents and indeed to OFSTED inspectors if necessary. The use of a single curriculum label such as 'careers education' is not necessarily synonymous with a singular

mode of delivery. Any label that describes the school's aims for this curriculum area would suffice; it could describe any number of approaches to
its delivery within the curriculum. The litmus test for a school is the extent
to which its current approaches prepare all pupils to maximize their life
chances as adults. Primary schools may find the following questions to be
a useful basis for reviewing careers education:

- is there a clear and commonly held **definition** of careers education in the
  school?
- do the essential elements of careers education receive sufficient **priority**
  in the curriculum?
- are these definitions and essential elements reflected in the school's curriculum **policies**?
- are there effective arrangements for the **management** and evaluation of
  careers education?
- is careers education included in the **staff development** programme?
- is there evidence of **a planned approach** to careers education, in the
  school development plan and schemes of work, for example?

Definition

The Department of Education and Science (DES) offer some useful definitions in *Careers Education and Guidance from 5–16: Curriculum Matters
10* (DES 1988). Career is used:

> to describe the variety of occupational roles which individuals will
> take throughout life. It includes: paid and self-employment; the dif-
> ferent occupations which a person may have over the years and
> periods of unemployment, and unpaid occupations, such as that of
> a student, voluntary worker or parent. All of these occupational roles
> are linked to the acquisition of qualifications, skills and experience.
> Guidance refers to activities which aim to help pupils as individuals
> to make choices and transitions which are appropriate for them. It
> is a continuous process through which young people are assisted in
> interrelating their growing understanding of the demands, respon-
> sibilities, opportunities and values of adult life. Guidance may be per-
> sonal, educational or vocational in nature but these aspects are not
> always distinct and shade into one another.

Priority

Defining and identifying 'careers education' (or whatever term the school
decides to call it) is an important step in asserting the priority the school
chooses to give to this area of the curriculum. This will also be signalled

by the extent to which parents and local employers are involved in discussions about the content of this curriculum and indeed may become key contributors to curriculum delivery. If careers education is to be prioritized in practice as well as in policy (see below) it will need to be made visible in the mainstream planning and management practices of the school. There is also a role for the LEA in underlining the importance of careers education in schools and acting as a buffer for schools against the pressures of national priorities. For example, Coventry Education Support and Advisory Service accompanied its careers education guidance to schools with the following message:

> At a time when there is overt acknowledgment of curriculum overload and when there are attempts to judge schools' performance on core and foundation subject results, the position of cross-curricular themes is vulnerable. I have no wish to add to the curriculum manageability problems which schools already face but I believe that we should hold fast to the concept of entitlement to a broad and balanced curriculum. I therefore hope that ... you will take the opportunity to build on the good work already being developed across the curriculum.
>
> (Coventry City Council 1993)

Policy

A policy is an important means of establishing the purposes of careers education and the framework within which it will take place with an indication of what will be covered at which key stage. The development of such a policy should involve wide consultation and regular review. It is likely that it will include statements under some or all of the following headings:

- aims and objectives
- management and organization
- resources
- curriculum, planning, development and review
- recording and reporting
- equal opportunities
- monitoring and evaluation
- teaching and learning styles
- staff development.

It is evident from this list of headings that in addition to stating clearly the main aims and objectives of careers education, the policy will also need to reflect key elements of other whole school policies such as equal opportunities. Her Majesty's Inspectorate (DES 1988: 11) asserts:

> Schools have a significant influence on the confidence aspirations and

career patterns of boys and girls, including pupils from ethnic minorities and those who have special needs whether long or short term. The images which young people form of themselves are influenced from the earliest years by the models presented by other people, in and out of schools, by the nature of the curriculum they are offered and by the range of choices available. Schools have a responsibility to ensure that negative or demoralising stereotypes, for example those restricting the sort of employment opportunities available to women, are not reinforced by pupils' reading and text books, by illustrations and display material. More than that they need to encourage realistically high aspirations in pupils of all abilities, aptitudes and backgrounds, and to provide an education which keeps open, for each individual, the widest possible range of career opportunities. Through the curriculum as a whole, schools need to ensure that pupils have equal access to and equal opportunities in, careers education and guidance, regardless of aptitude, ability, sex or ethnic background.

In addition to reflecting whole school policies within the careers education policy, it is also important that curriculum policies reflect the relevant features for that subject of careers education policy, for example how careers education will be taught through particular National Curriculum attainment targets and progammes of study. A cross-curricular policy must be expressed in ways that are consistent with its mode of delivery–that is, it should permeate the range of policies that inform the whole curriculum. Clearly this includes Personal and Social Education (PSE) and a whole range of aspects of the 'hidden' curriculum including pupil roles as classroom 'monitors', as helpers to younger children, in paired reading schemes, as lunchtime telephone operators, in bilingual support and 'induction mentoring' and as guides for visitors and so on.

Management

Schools need to have arrangements for the management and coordination of careers education across the curriculum. Although the detail of this will depend on the plan for curriculum delivery, management arrangements will need to ensure that staff are clear about their roles and responsibilities in relation to careers education. There may be one member of staff who has overall responsibility for key stage coordination, review and support, while others have responsibilities as curriculum leaders for building aspects of careers education into their subject planning and review. The head or deputy will need to ensure that policy is implemented consistently, particularly when adults other than teachers contribute to the programme. If careers education policy is to be successfully implemented appropriate resources will have to be earmarked annually in the school development plan.

Staff development

Most primary teachers will have mixed feelings about their role in teaching careers education at Key Stages One and Two. They will need opportunities to discuss the range of issues identified in this chapter, and these discussions will need to be planned and resourced on the same basis as other subject and cross-curricular areas, so that the priority attached by the school to careers education is reflected in the support given to staff. Guidance on approaches adopted by the school should also be available to other adults who contribute to the school's programme, visiting speakers from industry, members of the local community and the like.

A planned approach

Aims and objectives
Her Majesty's Inspectorate (DES 1988: 21) recommended that:

> During the primary and early secondary years, the curriculum should provide pupils with experiences which contribute to their growing knowledge and understanding of themselves and of a range of occupations and to the development of skills associated with choice and decision making, in addition to such basic skills as literacy, oracy and numeracy.

Her Majesty's Inspectorate urged primary schools to encourage the development of:

- qualities which enable pupils to adjust to and cope with change,
- self-confidence, a sense of personal worth and resilience in the face of set-back and disappointment,
- a positive attitude towards acquiring a range of skills, knowledge and understanding of adult life,
- a determination to make the most of one's talents and opportunities, through, for example, showing initiative and adopting an enterprising approach.

Curriculum planning
In primary schools it is evident that contributions to careers education and guidance will be made in the teaching of many subjects and aspects of the curriculum, in the values and attitudes of the teachers, in extra-curricular

activities and the variety of routines and events which contribute to school life. Such experiences, in different ways and to varying extents, contribute to young people's perceptions of adult and working life, of themselves and of others. Some experiences will be planned by the teacher, others will be unplanned but will be experienced in the context of the overall ethos and philosophy of the school; the status and role of support staff for example, and the way in which visitors to the school are received. Those aspects of careers education that can be planned into the primary curriculum can be delivered in a variety of ways. For example.

- as an extension of existing practice in Key Stage One, for example talking to adults about their work and role-play;
- through topics based on other cross-curricular themes, for example, PSE and Citizenship;
- through schemes of work based on the National Curriculum programmes of study which provide opportunities to find out about self, roles, work and changes;
- through topics primarily focused on the world of work which have clear objectives and which are well structured;
- through mini-enterprise and school-industry link activities;
- through particular approaches to classroom management, classroom organization and curriculum delivery;
- through involving children in the organization and work of the school.

Key Stage One

The National Curriculum Council (NCC) (1990) suggested that during the pre-school years children acquire an awareness of work in the home and their immediate neighbourhood. Children's impressions are formed by their parents, other adults whom they see working and media influences – particularly television. Their knowledge expands through new contacts and experiences. Increasingly, they notice similarities and differences between types of work; for example, jobs that require uniforms or particular vehicles. They notice features of work that they like and dislike, and these distinctions form the basis of their developing knowledge of self, roles, work and transition.

Key Stage Two

From years 3–6 pupils are expanding their awareness of adult working life. They know that work can be voluntary or paid. They appreciate the main reasons why people work and some of the effects of not working. They become aware of additional jobs which exist beyond their neighbourhood and begin to recognize the contribution that these make to the community. They begin to classify work according to features such as working with people or animals, or designing or making, and they form ideas about the jobs they might like to do and imagine themselves in work roles.

Some examples of careers education in schools in Coventry

The following examples illustrate some of the ways in which teachers in some Coventry schools have included careers education in the Key Stage One and Two curriculum:

Example 1: Careers education as an extension of existing practice in Key Stage One, such as talking to adults about their work and role play

This role-play activity involved the parallel infant classes of the deputy head and another teacher (years 1 and 2) and the children and teachers were used to working together. The activity session was planned to last an hour and a quarter and to take place each week. The children were grouped in threes with membership of the groups changing from week to week.

Each group was given a list of 12 role-play activities to choose from and a collection of resources to help them act out the situations, and the teachers moved from group to group discussing and developing ideas with them. The following conversation was recorded, by a teacher, in a group which was role-playing 'Mum goes to work. Dad takes children to the park':

Situation: with Lego the children had first constructed what were to be a house and an office. They were given a toy car and little wooden dolls.

Mum: OK. Let's have breakfast [to child] what do you want?
Teacher: Don't forget you have to go to work. Dad can make the breakfast.
Dad: But I've been working all night. I've just come back.
Teacher: No, you haven't got a job outside. Your wife works in an office. You can stay at home.
Dad: But I can still work at night.
Teacher: No, in this case pretend you haven't got a job outside.
Dad: OK then let me make breakfast.
Mum: All right, bye bye. [To child] Kiss, kiss. Bye dear. Oh, what do you want me to buy from the shops?
Teacher: Why not let Dad do the shopping? You go to the office.
Mum: Right. Bye bye [takes car to office].
Teacher: [To dad] What are you going to do now?

Dad: I don't know . . .
Child: Hm . . . We'll go shopping.
Teacher: Take the bus.
Dad: [Thinks] We'll walk.
Dad: [In the shop, to child] What do you want?
Child: Sweets, chocolate.
Dad: OK, here you are.
Teacher: But are they good for your teeth?
Dad: No . . . [to child] What do you want?
Child: Adidas shoes . . .
Mum: Oooh, they're spending all my money!
Teacher: Never mind, never mind . . . let's go home now.
Mum: All right . . . I'm home dear . . . oh . . . Let me get out of
          my coat . . . and scarf and gloves. Alright, what do you
          want for dinner?

Learning objectives including a focus on:

- increased understanding of the relationship between work and home roles;
- promoting confidence in achievements (in construction tasks);
- promoting pupils' confidence as facilitators, ensuring that the group is genuinely shared;
- ensuring that group discussions focus around alternative gender roles;
- negotiating and group decision making.

Example 2: Topics based on other cross-curricular themes such as PSE

Years 5 and 6 children were asked to think about and discuss in groups skills which they felt they had developed. Each child was asked to think of three sentences to describe their achievements, and three to describe their ambitions for the future. Some time was spent talking about this in preparation for the group discussions in order to clarify what was felt to constitute an achievement. At first the emphasis seemed to be purely on academic achievement and the teacher needed to encourage children to think in a wider sense. The teacher asked if there were any children who could speak more than one language or write in any language other than English. This question was greeted with enthusiasm and many members of the class were surprised to learn that there were a number in their class who could do both. They discussed physical achievements and it was recognized that the fastest runner in the class was a girl. They also talked about what other qualities were important such as being a good friend, helping at home and who could cook a good meal. Many boys became very animated about their culinary expertise.

The discussions about future ambitions were also interesting and although they focused on academic achievement they also included many resolves to be a more caring person! The teacher was pleasantly surprised at some of the responses from children and the challenges made to the more stereotypical roles. However, not all the children were entirely convinced that it was not 'cissy' for a boy to want to help his mum in the house more in the future. Below are listed some of the examples from the session which were included in pupils' Records of Achievement folders:

> I can speak two languages and write three
> I can cook spaghetti bolognese
> I can climb a big tree
> I can wash up and dry the dishes
> I will help more around the house
> I will go to university when I grow up
> I will have children when I grow up.

Learning objectives included a focus on:

- writing or drawing skills;
- speaking and listening skills;
- raising the self-esteem of all pupils;
- widening pupils' definition of achievement;
- identifying skills which can be built on and shared;
- looking forward to the future.

Example 3: Schemes of work based on the National Curriculum programmes of study which provide opportunities to find out about self, roles, work and changes

As part of the humanities curriculum, staff in years 5 and 6 planned a topic on migration in which all children traced their family backgrounds including the arrival of their family in England. The children had all been born in England but all of their families had originated from elsewhere, such as Scotland, India, Pakistan and the Caribbean. The children considered the situations faced by immigrants arriving in new countries, including racism and low pay, and many of them could relate experiences from their own family. They became increasingly interested in experiences of racism and in how black people in particular deal with various forms of oppression. The lives of Martin Luther King, Harriet Tubman, the Rani of Jhansi and Nelson Mandela were studied using materials from a variety of sources.

For example, the Rani was an Indian Queen who fought against the British when they refused to acknowledge her adopted son as her legitimate heir. Her story was given a present-day relevance by being presented as a play within a play set in present-day Coventry. A Coventry mother told the story to her two children, a boy and a girl, who squabbled about boys' and girls' roles and duties about the house. As the mother told the story it came to life and demonstrated to the audience that a woman could be a leader and a warrior. Serena aged 10, who played the part of Rani, wrote about the play:

> I learnt a lot from the Rani of Jhansi. I thought it was a big experience for me and I think it taught us all that the girls and boys are equal . . . my ambition is to become a lawyer and some people think that to be a lawyer you have to be a boy. But if I am affected by this when I grow up I will stand up for what I believe in . . . But I will have to work hard.
>
> (Millman and Shipton 1994: 155)

Learning objectives included a focus on:

- reasons for and effects of low pay strategies for dealing with sex and race discrimination including the law;
- similarities and differences between self and others;
- ways of adapting to change;
- learning from adult role models in the community.

Example 4: Topics primarily focused on the world of work which have clear objectives and are well structured

The activity began with groups of years 5 and 6 children listing as many different types of jobs as possible. This became very competitive with children accusing each other of copying and the teacher had to be very careful to play down the element of 'how many could you think of?' in favour of 'let's have some *unusual* jobs'.

Each group nominated their own scribe and this in itself caused some problems of individuals fighting over marker pens! At feedback time the teacher carefully chose the group with the least number of jobs on their list and asked others to tick them off as they were read out.

When each group had offered their suggestions the teacher asked them to look at their list again and indicate by the use of a colour code which were 'male' and which were 'female' occupations. It was interesting to note the language they used in describing the jobs. Policeman, milkman, army man, dustbin man, lollypop lady and dinner lady were all there along with many more gender specific terms.

As children worked in the groups there was some discussion about the possibility that certain jobs could be done by members of both sexes. The teacher intervened at times to challenge their decisions. She approached this by suggesting that perhaps one day she woke up and decided to be a window cleaner. What would stop her doing this? The responses were amazing: Girls can't be window cleaners because they don't like heights; Boys can't be nurses because they have to be doctors; Girls can't be mechanics because they wear dresses, and they don't like getting dirty; Girls can't be astronauts because they haven't had any practice being weightless!; Boys can't be cooks because they are too lazy and they can't wash up. There were some heated exchanges particularly between two members of one class. This had to be handled sensitively as the teacher felt one boy was becoming upset and confused. This had partly to do with the role models in his own home and his standing with his peers. Despite this the teacher felt that the activities were successful because children were able to express feelings about role models, were engaged in discussion and some found that their views were being challenged.

Learning objectives included a focus on:

• increasing knowledge of a wider range of jobs;
• examining some of the reasons for the sex-segregated labour market;
• understanding different points of view;
• exploring the influence of role models;
• negotiating roles within a group;
• extending vocabulary associated with 'careers'.

Example 5: Careers education through mini-enterprise and school industry link activities

A six-week school-based module was devised which included a half-day visit to the Rover Group Education Partnership Centre. The *Types and Uses of Materials* (Coventry Rover Group Educational Partnership 1993) module is built around Key Stage One requirements of the National Curriculum in science.

The module started by the class looking at materials which were already familiar to them. Activities included looking at the variety of materials used in school, going on metal hunts, rubber hunts or plastic hunts and recording their findings, making models with household materials and discussing the suitability of materials for specific tasks.

Before the visit to the Rover centre the class talked about where cars come from, their similarities and differences, who makes them and where they can be bought from. There was discussion about the companies that make the cars and the people who work in them. A survey was carried out to discover if any of the children's relations worked for a car firm including Rover. The half-day visit to the Rover Centre included six different activities: the 'feely' box of car components; guess the car part; squash and smell; sorting materials; materials hunt and policeman's bum. The children watched various materials and components being tested by different people, and the most popular activity was the policeman's bum test where a computer programmed machine simulated the action of a sixteen-stone policeman sitting on a car seat 10,000 times!

Learning objectives included a focus on:

- promoting a favourable image of the manufacturing industry, especially engineering, to children and their parents;
- motivating children by showing that work and skills acquired in school are used in the world of work;
- investigating the role of technology in the workplace;
- broadening children's knowledge of occupations;
- widening children's experience by offering learning activities in a different setting but with the security of their own teachers;
- promoting equal opportunities by providing positive role models in terms of gender and race.

Example 6: Careers education through particular approaches to classroom management, classroom organization and curriculum delivery

We need to group children for different reasons, but should the teacher tell the children which group they should be with? This teacher decided that imposed groups were not really serving a purpose – she was not enabling the children to make thoughtful choices as to which group to work with. So she devised a set of criteria which she thought might enable children to make these choices. The questions posed were these:

- Are you in a group of girls and boys sometimes?
- Is there any time when a single-sex group might be appropriate?
- Do you always have to be in the same group as your best friend?
- Do you include in your group people who are quiet?
- Do these quiet people get the chance to be group leader?
- Do you include in your group people who might have difficulty with writing and spelling?
- Do these people get the chance to be group leader?
- How can we support each other in a group?
- Is there someone in the group who always tries to take over? How can we stop this person doing that?

These questions were discussed and a wide range of ideas emerged. Many children thought that mixed groups of girls and boys were a good idea because you learned to get along with each other and find things in common. The girls wanted single-sex groups for technology because they felt the boys interfered and tried to take over. A definite 'no' to being with your best friend all the time emerged as the children felt this was too limiting.

The question of shy people and people with writing and reading difficulties was approached very carefully. One answer the children came up with for helping shy people to speak out was for everyone to write a sentence down and then read it out so that everyone got a turn. Some quiet people worked in twos within the group at the beginning and gave each other confidence. The important thing about this discussion was that it allowed children to make choices, be independent, take responsibility and be resourceful. They had to make decisions and be sensitive to the needs of others.

After the discussion the teacher was very heartened when one very shy boy actually came up and said he would love to speak out in the class but he was too shy. She felt he had taken the first and hardest step by saying this and, asking his permission first, shared his comments with the class – the children responded with helpful comments, such as suggesting that Phillip sat near the teacher in discussions, so that he could say things quietly until he got used to speaking out.

Learning objectives included a focus on:

- decision making;
- working as a team;
- speaking to a group;
- self-appraisal.

Conclusion

While many young people will in future choose to remain near to the locality in which they have grown up, a significant number will move into new localities in Britain and in Europe. Part of the education of young children is a progressive and supported extension of their boundaries and widening of their horizons, giving them both the skills and confidence to move beyond what is already safe and familiar.

This chapter has demonstrated that today's primary school children will, as young adults living at the beginning of the next millennium, need to chart their paths through new and uncertain territory in both their working and personal lives. As teachers we must take their futures seriously from a young age and be sure that we not only equip them to cope with the transitions they will need to make but also give them the confidence to gain access to and shape the world in which they will he participating.

Throughout their lives they are likely to move through a variety of occupational roles – paid and unpaid – and live in a variety of personal circumstances. For some, there will be more barriers put in their way and more hurdles to overcome than others. The children we teach have much to learn from the knowledge and understanding we have gained through our own experiences, and of course the experiences of other adults; but it is not enough to leave this to chance. Children are entitled to receive a programme of careers education in the primary school that is carefully planned, albeit broadly defined and flexibly delivered. It is only by planning our approach across the whole school that we can be sure we are offering children consistent help in making sense of the adult world and preparing them to make the most of their future place within it.

Acknowledgements

The examples were developed in the following Coventry schools: Edgewick Community Primary School; Halsgrave Church of England School; Southfields Primary School; Henry Parkes Primary School and Howes Primary School in association with the Rover Group Education Partnership Centre. The accounts of practice were described by the following teachers with support from former members of the Curriculum Support Team: Brian Morley; Barbara Thomas; Nancy Starrit; Carol Laye and Helen Brown with Jane Wilding. Thanks are also due to Janice Wale for her helpful comments on an earlier draft.

References

Coventry City Council (1993) Letter to school from the Chief Adviser. Coventry: Coventry City Council.

Coventry Rover Group Educational Partnership (CRGP) (1993) *Types and Uses of Materials*. Coventry: Rover Group.

Dearing, Sir, R. (1994) *The National Curriculum and its Assessment* (the Dearing Report). London: National Curriculum Council.

Department of Education and Science (DES) (1988) *Careers Education and Guidance from 5–16: Curriculum Matters 10*. London: DES.

Department of Employment (DoE) (1994a) *Competitiveness*. White Paper, May. London: DoE.

Department of Employment (DoE) (1994b) *Labour Market and Skill Trends 1994/5*. London: DoE.

Department of Education and Science (DES) (1988) *Education Reform Act (1988)*. London: HMSO.

Jones, T. (1993) *Britain's Ethnic Minorities*. London(?): Policy Studies Institute.

Millman, V. and Shipton, S. (1994) *Cross-Curricular Contexts, Themes and Dimensions*. Volume 4 of *Gender Issues in Cultural Diversity and the Curriculum*. London: Falmer Press.

National Curriculum Council (NCC) (1990) *Careers Education and Guidance: Curriculum Guidance 6*. London: NCC.

Office for Standards in Education (OFSTED) (1994) *The Handbook for the Inspection of Schools*. London: HMSO.

Watts, T. (1993) Connecting curriculum to work: past patterns, current initiatives and future issues, in J. Wellinton (ed.) *The Work-Related Curriculum*. London: Kogan Page.

Useful sources

Agnew, D. (1992) Careers education and guidance in K. Meyers (ed.) *Genderwatch*. Cambridge: Cambridge University Press.

Millman, V. (1985) Breadwinning and babies, in G. Weiner (ed.) *Just a Bunch of Girls: Feminist Approaches to Schooling*. Milton Keynes: Open University Press.

8

JOHN SIRAJ-BLATCHFORD
and LINA PATEL

Understanding environmental education for the primary classroom

Editors' introduction

John Siraj-Blatchford and Lina Patel's chapter, focuses upon children's work developed to engage with people and communities, and upon buildings and industrialization. Environmental Studies is offered as a means of unifying studies of science, technology, history, geography and society within local contexts that allow children to begin to develop their understandings from an experiential base. Readers are introduced to an 'ecocentric' approach to environmental issues, an approach that puts the interrelationship between the various constituents of our 'living' planet on an equal footing rather than seeing ourselves as the key component.

The authors outline and explore the key components of environmental education and relate these to practical examples for the classroom. Both macro (societal and global) and micro (local and individual) contexts are considered in discussing the appropriateness of technological innovations as well as the values that are inherent within them. Particular attention is placed on children working cooperatively in their own learning community. It is suggested that these experiences may then be extended to provide a grounding for understanding the global issues.

Introduction: understanding ecocentrism

> *We know that the white man does not understand our ways. He is a stranger who comes in the night, and takes from the land whatever he needs. The earth is not his friend, but his enemy, and when he's conquered it he moves on. He kidnaps the earth from his children. His appetite will devour the earth and leave behind a desert. If all the beasts were gone, we would die from a great loneliness of the spirit, for whatever happens to the beasts also happens to us. All things are connected. Whatever befalls the earth, befalls the children of the earth.*
>
> (Chief Seattle 1855)

Complex questions regarding integrated and interdependent ecological systems have often been reduced to the limited economic or technical concerns of specialists. The fragmentary nature of contemporary thinking has led to a breakdown in both ecological and cultural integrity that has in turn reduced the ability of both global (macro) and local (micro) systems to self-regulate (Stirling 1990). At an individual, institutional and social level, actions that are taken in our personal self-interests at the expense of the interests of others are now widely recognized as the basic cause of environmental contamination and the current threat to the planet's future. In a sense, people pollute, are careless about the environment and choose to adopt non-sustainable technologies due to a failure of community. Even more fundamentally, within the Green movement, and for many others committed to ecological principles, 'anthropocentrism', the inclination to regard humankind as the centre and aim of the universe represents the most destructive tendency humanity has yet contrived. Perhaps paradoxically, this chapter may itself be considered by some to be tainted by such a perspective. It is actually informed by a deep conviction that the necessary short-term changes in values and behaviours will only occur through the mobilization of self-interest. Any such consciousness will itself only be founded upon social critique. The move towards a more 'ecocentric' future, where natural systems are respected and protected is in fact ultimately a speculative project involving a change of popular perceptions equal to any envisaged by Castaneda (1970) or Pirsig (1976). Anthropocentrism has led science to 'split things up' and study them in isolation and the National Curriculum has (significantly) split the curriculum into separate subjects. The curriculum thus reproduces the problem, preparing individuals for a future as specialists rather than providing an education for environmentally conscious democrats. We have increasingly lost the capability of understanding, and acting upon, the holistic interacting system that sustains us.

The Gaia hypothesis

James Lovelock's Gaia hypothesis (1979) suggests that the earth's living and non-living systems form an inseparable whole. According to the hypothesis, this complex global interdependent system is self-regulating. The living organisms and chemical processes of our planet 'naturally' adapt to preserve the environment and maintain ecological equilibrium. Increasingly popular, Lovelock's hypothesis emphasizes interdependence and displaces humanity from the centre of ecological concern. However, as Dobson (1990) points out, on the face of it the Gaia hypothesis suggests that on a planetary scale there is no fundamental ecological threat and that given the self-regulatory processes 'life is, as Lovelock (1979) puts it "near immortal"':

> It is now generally accepted that man's industrial activities are fouling the nest and pose a threat to the total life of the planet which grows more ominous every year. Here, however, I part company with conventional thought. It may be that the white-hot rash of our technology will in the end prove destructive and painful for our own species, but the evidence for accepting that industrial activities either at their present level or in the immediate future may endanger the life of Gaia as a whole, is very weak indeed.
>
> (Lovelock 1979: 107)

The question is of course, whose threat to survival are we considering? It may well be that Gaia's power of survival is such that humanity is ultimately proven to be ecologically expendable! Humanity may ultimately be under greater immediate threat from the side-effects of Gaia's self-regulatory mechanisms, triggered to ensure ecological equilibrium, than from the direct effects of its own industrial pollution and environmental mismanagement. In compensating for atmospheric pollution, for example, a change of climate could be triggered that is good for the system as a whole while fatal for humankind as a species. In recent years we have had widely reported cases that would seem to corroborate the Gaia hypothesis. Many environmental scientists have been extremely surprised at the capacity of the ecosystem to deal with severe cases of oil pollution such as that created in the Iraqi invasion of Kuwait.

Environmental education

From whatever quarter they come, the dangers of ignoring the environment are now widely recognized. Gro Haslem Broudtland, in his Chairman's foreword to the report of the World Commission on Environment and Development (WCED) (1987: iv) called for 'a vast campaign of education, debate, and public participation' to achieve 'changes in attitudes, in social values and in aspirations'. Rudolf Bahro (1982) suggests that the 'minority world's'[1] obsession with commodities deflects attention from the full implications of their dominant economic model. This is relevant education for economic and industrial understanding as set out in *Curriculum Guidance Four: Education for Economic Understanding* (CG4) (NCC 1990a) and is consistent with the arguments put forward by Alistair Ross in Chapter 6. Redclift (1984: 4) cites the work of Gorz, who argues that mass unemployment is endemic to industrial society and that 'the manner in which the abolition of work is to be managed and socially implemented constitutes the central political issue of the coming decades'. Millman argues a similar case in her discussion of careers education and guidance in relation to *Curriculum Guidance Six: Careers Education and Guidance* (CG6) (NCC 1990b) (Chapter 7).

Curriculum Guidance Seven: Environmental Education (CG7) (NCC 1990c) suggests that environmental education may be thought of as comprising of three linked components:

- 'education *about* the environment' (as knowledge);
- 'education *for* the environment' (as values, attitudes, positive, action);
- 'education *in* or *through* the environment' (as a resource).

In the following pages we shall attempt to provide specific guidance in each of these areas.

The primary years

Research shows that children with a high self-regard tend to be more altruistic, generous and sharing. As suggested in other chapters, we can help children develop such positive self-images through enhanced communication, cooperative games and by involving them in the educational process. It is never too early to teach children about interdependence.

Much of the research into how children think and learn about maps and spatial awareness fails to consider children's differing experiences or consider issues of equity. For instance, Jahoda's research cited in Bale (1987) concluded that children from middle-class backgrounds outscored working-class children in tests designed to show conceptualization of the nature of Glasgow and its relationship with Scotland and Britain. Such research does little to challenge the crude application of Piagetian developmental stages or to contribute to our understanding of how children learn. Margaret Donaldson (1978) has argued that when a task is in context and meaningful, children can begin to decentre, and see situations from different points of view. Bruner (1986) suggested that children can be taught any subject in an honest way regardless of their age.

Bale (1987) also cites research by Boareman and Towner (1979) who argue that innate ability may account for boys out-performing girls in spatial ability. Any writer who fails to challenge this view is actively perpetuating notions of gender superiority and inferiority. Bale also cites research that suggests that cultural factors are a more convincing reason for girls being held back in their spatial development. However, in failing to draw any conclusions, this treatment of the issue continues to pathologize the family and fails to examine the possible significance of education. The evidence actually suggests that when given active encouragement and opportunity girls prove to be at least as capable as their male peers in these as in other educational contexts. While it is recognized that sexual stereotyping often determines children's choice of clothes or toys, it is less often noted that the particular behaviours expected of boys and girls mean that girls are often disadvantaged in developing such skills. This makes it essential that the curriculum on offer gives girls access and active encouragement to develop these skills. Lego may thus be used to build models of the local high street, with shops, homes, streets and cars. It will be in *structured* play contexts, utilizing such models that children are given the opportunity to plan, create and think about the needs and wants of the people in their community. A visit to the local market or supermarket, a canal, a house, a street or a place of worship fits into a range of topics and enables children to build on their mental maps, develop their spatial ability and think critically about their environment and the wider world.

Deception–demonstration–debate

As children come to recognize the relevance of wider contexts Abraham and colleagues' (1990) model of 'deception, demonstration and debate' may be increasingly adopted to inform our practice.

When some change, some new biotechnology for example, is introduced and justified in terms of benefits that are unrealized or result in some harmful effects, this should be regarded as a 'deception'. The term is used here without any implication of intention. Clearly the gravity of some environmental changes that have already been introduced (for example, those concerned with radioactive discharge) have been such as to make any concern regarding individual culpability marginal. Abraham and Lacey suggest that the 'demonstration' or uncovering of 'deception' may be achieved through scientific research or through insider whistle blowing, and that public debate should follow in an attempt to achieve a reconciliation of the inevitably opposing views. The deception–demonstration–debate model is thus offered as a pedagogic device that relates education to the concepts of public debate and democracy at two levels:

1 in appealing to democracy and openness, it provides the educator with an important legitimation for teaching controversial environmental issues, and
2 as a powerful analytical tool, the model provides a critical alternative to the 'accumulation of knowledge' model that currently dominates and stifles real education.

As Abraham and colleagues (1990: 195) put it: 'In other words it could be relevant to building new understandings and a new intelligence vital to our collective future'.

Huckle (1990) provides a useful account of the environmental components that need to be incorporated into the curriculum:

The components of environmental education in the new social curriculum

Knowledge of the natural environment and its potential for human use

Environmental education should be based on a knowledge of major ecological systems, the processes which sustain them and their vulnerability to human modification. Scientists and geographers should develop appropriate knowledge and cultivate a sense of wonder and respect for nature.

A theoretical and practical grasp of appropriate technology

Lessons in Science and Craft, Design and Technology, should consider the environmental and social impacts of technology and develop pupils' theoretical and practical understanding of appropriate technology.

A sense of history and a knowledge of the impact of changing social formations on the environment

Pupils should understand the impact of changing economies and societies on the natural world. They should understand how environments are socially constructed, how social relations shape environmental relations, and how landscapes and environments reflect technology and social organisation. Additionally, they should appreciate the potential benefits of sustainable development in the contemporary world.

An awareness of class conflict

Pupils should be aware that rich and poor share unequally in the gains from our past and present use of nature, in control over economic development, and in the social costs of ecological disruption and the extent of environmental protection. People have frequently challenged the logic and costs of unbridled development and these issues deserve a place in the curriculum.

Political literacy

The state is generally the arbitrator in disputes over the social use of nature and the environment. Pupils should develop 'political literacy' so that they are able to understand and participate in environmental politics. Appropriate knowledge, skills and attitudes should be developed through real or simulated involvement with environmental issues at all scales, from the local to the global. Due attention should be given to the social use of nature and environmental politics in societies organised on different principles than our own.

An awareness of alternative social and environmental features and the political strategies whereby they are likely to be realised

Pupils should consider alternative forecasts about society and the environment, the desirability of a range of environmental possibilities, and the feasibility of bringing them about.

An understanding of environmental ideology and consumer lifestyles

Pupils should study the environmental movement and relate its beliefs and strategies to wider political philosophies and programmes. They should recognise the consequences of consumer lifestyles on the environment.

Involvement in real issues

Pupils should be encouraged to identify for themselves practical ways in which they can work for a more sustainable relationship with the natural world. This is likely to involve changes in lifestyle, involvement in community projects, and possible political action.

Balance

Environmental education should be balanced and avoid indoctrination, at the same time introducing pupils to a wide range of topics and ideas. While we should be committed to justice, rationality and democracy, rather than to a form of neutrality which leaves existing patterns of power and privilege undisturbed, we should protect students from our own powers of persuasion and cultivate tentativeness and constructive scepticism.

Optimism

If we are not to overwhelm pupils with the world's problems, we should teach in a spirit of optimism. We should build environmental success stories into our curriculum and develop awareness of sources of hope in a world where new and appropriate technologies now offer liberation for all.

(Huckle 1990, Fig. 10.1: 158–9)

Cultivating appropriate knowledge and a 'sense of wonder'

The National Curriculum orders for science and geography provide a context for developing much of the knowledge and understanding required in this area. Environmental studies provides a clear context for curriculum integration. In Chapters 5 and 7 Epstein and Millman have considered the future role of women in society and it is important to recognize that the feminist movement has contributed significantly in focusing greater public attention upon the shortcomings of modern reductionary scientific thinking (Harding 1991). Links between an opposition to nuclear armament, environmental action and feminism have also been characteristic of developments within the Green movement across Europe. While an association of 'women' with 'nature' has been emphasized by some feminists this may only serve to reinforce popular stereotypes and facilitate patriarchal domination. There can be little doubt however, that the case does demonstrate that masculinity requires redefinition. If we are to achieve a sustainable future, then cooperation and social interaction must be prioritized over aggression and individualism. Given the degree of cultural contamination in this respect, some form of attitude remediation and the development of a 'sense of wonder' about nature is especially required for boys.

Consumer lifestyles and class conflict

If children are to become aware and conscious of their environment, discussion and activities must first start from their experiences, and these may then lead on to looking at the lives and environments of people in the wider world. They may begin by discussing the clothes they wear for different occasions, events and weather conditions. They could discuss their own clothes when they were babies and now, which will enable them to identify the changes that have taken place, the function of clothes in relation to who wears what, why and when. This can lead on to looking at and discussing what we wear on special occasions, on birthdays, at different festivals, or what is worn in hot, cold and windy weather.

Most significantly, for children to understand the issues involved in environmental studies they will need to be taught the critical concept of technological 'appropriateness'. In the early stages this can most effectively be accomplished by using illustrations from the children's *own* experience. They can fruitfully discuss what the most 'appropriate' way is of drying clothes. Is it a washing line, a clothes-horse in front of the fire or an electric tumble dryer? What are the advantages and disadvantages? Would the answer be the same in another climate? What is the most appropriate writing technology for school students? What is the most appropriate footwear? Surely it is not asking too much to achieve a level of technological literacy sufficient to recognize the folly of severely disrupting the family's budgetary arrangements for the sake of a pair of trainers? Increasingly students can be encouraged to consider appropriateness in other people's terms, the aim being to encourage empathy rather than sympathy.

Addressing issues of environmental education through the study of the local area is one way that enables children to work from the concrete to the abstract. The careful selection of an area will enhance any topic and the use of old and new maps, photos, posters and videos, along with information from books and interviews with people will enhance the children's direct experience and support their learning. As we shall see, the main concepts to examine will often be concerned with changes in the built environment, with the causes and consequences of these changes and the division of labour involved.

For instance, when studying canals, children may be invited to discuss issues of conflict, the struggle between the use of canals, roads and railways and the cause and consequences of these developments. The children may also examine the similarities and differences between canals and rivers and why the need arose to build the canals. This should enable them to think about the impact of industrialization and the need to transport raw materials quickly from the colonies to various inland manufacturing sites. Children may also be able to study issues of power and authority in relation to those who built the canal. Who were the navigators? Where did they come from? This would provide a context for studying the potato famine and colonial Ireland.

Political literacy and involvement in real issues

As the Schools Council (1975: 4) project on ethics and environment suggested:

> Effective environmental education cannot rely on appeals to the conscience, to responsibility to fellows and to posterity ... To become interested in any environmental matter most students need to see how it affects their personal position ...

As suggested in the guidance document (CG7), learning about the environment should enable children to develop a sense of their location in relation to the wider world, and:

> First hand experience is an essential part of helping pupils to develop a personal response to the environment and to gain an awareness of environmental issues. This can start in the school itself, in the grounds and immediate locality, progressing to visits to more distant, contrasting localities in the United Kingdom, and in other countries.
> (NCC 1990c: 12)

The study of the local area can be a study in its own right and it might provide a starting point for further work or be incorporated within virtually any topic in the primary curriculum. Visits enable children to develop critical awareness and understanding of their social environment. However, unless careful groundwork is laid, children can get confused about location, which can mean that their understanding about the environment might not lead to the desirable goal of independent thinking. This confusion does not mean that children do not understand or that the concepts are too difficult, as many teachers influenced by crude Piagetian principles might suspect, but rather that the task needs to be broken down further and children need to be able to build on their existing knowledge to further their understanding.

A focus on the journey from home to school may provide a starting point for children to be thinking, discussing and drawing maps of their local area. Local issues may be identified and campaigns entered into. The potential has been demonstrated all over the country when children have been mobilized to 'save their school' from closure. Children are enthusiastic recyclers and this potential has barely been tapped. Children are also often acutely conscious of and concerned about fairness and injustice. John Siraj-

Blatchford's chapter on citizenship (Chapter 2) provides a number of strategies for developing children's involvement.

Many schools have focused on the playground as an environmental topic and have employed surveys to find out what children like and dislike about their playground. Children can conduct their own surveys, and such work has sometimes resulted in a code of conduct being compiled to ensure that bullying and racist and sexist abuse are dealt with. Often quiet areas are created and ball games confined to given sections. This can lead to looking at the green areas around the school and in the wider environment, leading to looking at children's experiences around the world. *Nowhere to Play* by Kurusa (1981) is based on the true story of the children of the barrio San Jose de la Urbana, Caracas, who wanted a place to play.

Appropriate technology

It is now widely recognized that the introduction of a new technology creates winners and losers (Layton 1991, 1992). Women, the disabled, ethnic minorities and majority world cultures are systematically dominated and disenfranchised socially, economically and culturally by the dominant technological forms (Siraj-Blatchford 1994).

In arguing that design and technology education should be relevant to all and can be used to challenge negative stereotypes, Makiya and Rogers (1992: 13) write:

> Since the design and technology profile component has such a strong emphasis on evaluation (AT4) [National Curriculum Attainment Target 4] and identifying and satisfying human need (AT1) [National Curriculum Attainment Target 1], and because value judgments are very strong aspects of both of these areas, it is necessary for teachers to consider how pupils build these value judgments and the factors that influence these. Gender and culture are two of these factors. Culture can also include peer culture, and social and economic cultures apart from historic and geographic factors.

The technological products that we encounter today are the product of value judgements made in the past; 'hardened history' as it has been called. An essential element of an education in design and technology thus involves some understanding of the range of value options and the reasons for choices between them, that have empowered the technological process in previous times and which are doing so today. The wording of AT4 (DES 1990), with its reference to 'an evaluation of the processes of Design and Technology in other times and cultures' is intended to ensure attention to this point. It is a fundamental economic truth that technological innovation always requires investment. This may be in terms of industrial investment capital, or in simple terms of the time dedicated to solving the problem or satisfying the relevant needs or opportunities. At an individual level we recognize that a new filing system may improve our working efficiency considerably. Yet without the investment of time, without someone else doing our other work for the time it takes to set up the system it cannot be implemented. In the same way large-scale technological changes and 'industrial revolutions' have only been achieved when time and resources have been invested in individuals or whole classes of people that have been released from the immediate labours of feeding themselves and their families. Historically this has largely been achieved through class and gender domination, colonial exploitation and slavery. Rapid technological developments have thus always created benefits for some at the expense of others. Children can be taught through real practical projects that are developed to improve the school environment that cooperative organization provides an alternative means to achieve investment.

Technological innovations are successful when the values are congruent between the designer and the consumer. Technologies would always be rejected or become obsolete when these values were non-congruent if it were not for the fact that they are often imposed. Nobel (1979) has described how technologies are often regarded as 'irreducible brute facts'. This may be most clearly illustrated in the case of wheelchair access, yet there are many other, often more subtle examples. The so-called 'Green Revolution', which has meant high yield varieties of grain have made farmers dependent upon the provision of seeds, pesticides and fertilizers, provides a good example of technological imperialism and shows how the consumer sometimes has no free choice, and how technologies can change social relations. It has impoverished small peasant farmers and turned them into landless labourers who are often unable to afford to buy the product themselves (Levidow 1987).

Taylor and Jenkins (1989) provide some valuable resources for teaching the concept of 'appropriateness', including the case of an evangelical Christian donor agency that provided a well-drilling rig with a Christian text attached to it. Children could debate whether a charity should impose their values on recipients. Another case shows how, while supporting a project marketing banana chips a development agency introduced divisive competition in a community. Others show how 'inappropriate' technologies can be unwittingly introduced, and all of the cases show what is at stake when individuals and groups exert their power to impose their technologies on others. As the authors say in explaining the title of their book:

The poor of the world are still getting poorer; there is need of some urgency. Urgency, nevertheless, can be a problem itself. TIME MUST

BE TAKEN TO LISTEN. Before an answer is volunteered, the question must be understood. Before an intervention is made, its full relevance must be considered.

(Taylor and Jenkins 1989: 1)

Another source of progressive material is provided by Pierre Gillet's *Small is Difficult: The Pangs and Success of Small Boat Technology Transfer in South India* (1985). Again the problems of uncritical technology transfer are illustrated, although in this case the story has a happy ending.

A 'sense of history'

By critically examining the past we may be better equipped to plan a more sustainable future. The study of buildings probably represents the most common context for environmental education in the primary school. Just like any other technological product, buildings are expressions of cultural needs and values. The Eiffel tower was built to impress other European countries and draw investment into French engineering companies at the time of the French Centennial exposition in 1889. The British built the huge prefabricated steel and glass structure Crystal Palace for the same reasons in 1851. Children may study and create models that incorporate the design features of what Rapport (1980) has referred to as 'folk architecture' as well as architecture from 'the grand tradition'. The degree to which buildings may be historically misinterpreted may be illustrated by the case of the first English homes built by the Anglo-Saxon 'barbarians' who invaded Britain in the 5th century. The walls were made of wattle and daub; that is, from branches packed with mud and turf to make them solid and weather resistant. The roofing was thatch. Historians used to think that the use of huts like this meant that the people who built them were unsophisticated, but the buildings actually represent a very appropriate design. The Anglo-Saxons were on the move all the time, so they needed a design that was easily constructed from common materials. English historians might have thought that they were primitive because they didn't understand what the German archaeological term for the houses meant; the Germans called them *grubenhaus*, meaning house with a pit. One of the problems that the Anglo-Saxons had with their design was in providing enough headroom, which they solved by digging down. The English historians called these houses 'grub-huts' and thought that the people who lived in them must be scavengers. We now know that the Anglo-Saxons were perfectly capable of sophisticated designs because we have evidence of their cleverly designed ships and of their communal halls, which were based upon the hull design of the ships and were built in each village.

To understand why buildings look the way they do children need to recognize that the form that folk architecture has taken depends on a complex mixture of factors such as: climate and the need for shelter; the availability of materials; construction skills; economics; the need for defence, religion and family structure. Despite the contrary suggestions of some historians, the form of very few buildings can be explained by any *one* of these factors. Shelter represents a basic human need and houses built all over the world reflect the need to keep the elements out. Beyond that, the form a building takes depends upon the specific needs and opportunities being addressed by its designer.

Children can build models that show the various qualities and features exhibited in the built environment. They should learn that when people change their way of life it would be wrong to assume that this is always for a 'higher' economic level. While we may often assume a development of standards from tent to hut to house, history suggests that the reality is actually more complex. With the introduction of the horse, the Cheyenne, for example, gave up their permanent villages of semi-subterranean houses and became nomads living in tepees. They gave up agriculture in order to hunt. Nomadic people who share equivalent economic circumstances use a variety of building forms; the Mongols developed the Yurt, the Tibetans a hexagonal tent. There are a number of forms of Arab tent, and some native Americans adopted the tepee while others developed much more substantial, yet still mobile, wooden houses. While the site chosen for building has often been significant in determining a settlement this has often been exaggerated. Even when defence has not been an issue people have sometimes built their homes close together simply because they are gregarious. The form that buildings take has sometimes been influenced by the need for defence but symbolism and other values are also significant. Hence the Masai built to defend their cattle yet in the Cameroon the need for defence was handled differently because granaries rather than cattle were valued.

The built environment may be studied in a historical and local context. Taking the Victorian period as an example, and using the local area as a starting point, children's awareness can be raised regarding the evidence that still exists; not only the architecture, but other aspects such as street furniture and transport. From this a number of themes can be explored, such as that of change. By comparing and contrasting the built environment in different periods, children can formulate their own questions to be investigated or exchanged with another group. Children would learn how the landscape changed quite significantly during the Victorian period and be encouraged to think about, and ask, why and how.

Looking closely at a Victorian household, children can investigate the roles and hierarchy of the people in the house, from the servants, the chimney sweep and the children, to the owners of the house. By examining photographs or visiting Victorian factory buildings, they may consider the images of children and people in the factories and various source materials may be supplied to provide accounts of different people's experiences at the time. Children will learn about the conditions the factory workers had to endure and this will lead to addressing issues of their own rights, and the implications of not having them. They will learn about Victorian living and working conditions, and the struggles that led to the passing of the factory acts to ensure better conditions. The struggles of the match-stick girls and their strike also provide good material. They might also learn about the experiences of those living in the colonies and plantations of the Empire during the period, and the effects upon their environment and conditions may be compared.

For Key Stage Two the revised history curriculum remains fairly prescriptive, but environmental education may be included, in the manner described above, through the core history units. Other historical periods provide as rich a potential for developing such critical comparative understandings. In an article in *Scientific American*, Donald Hill (1991) provides valuable illustrations of mechanical engineering in the medieval Near East. It has perhaps been too easy in the past to ignore the fact that in the 10th century Baghdad's population amounted to something like 1.5 million. Cities such as Córdoba, Cairo and Samarkand dwarfed other European capitals such as London and Paris at this time, and these vast urban centres put great demands on agriculture and distribution. As Hill says: 'These, in turn, depended on technology for supplying irrigation water to the fields and for processing the crops into foodstuffs (Hill 1991: 64).

The Islamic innovations that Hill identifies are significant and clearly demonstrate the ethnocentrism of historical accounts of the so-called 'dark ages'. The article includes illustrations of a 7th-century Islamic vertical axis windmill and a pump first described in Ibn al-Razzaz al-Jazari's *Book of Knowledge of Ingenious Mechanical Devices*, a text completed in Diyar Bakr in Upper Mesopotamia in 1206. The pump converted rotary to reciprocating motion and is a remarkable example of a double-acting pump with true suction pipes. The effects of such innovations as the windmill, first introduced from the Islamic world by returning crusaders, may help children to appreciate the degree and nature of human achievement and global interdependence today.

Environmental futures and ideology

If we accept Lovelock's account of Gaia as a working hypothesis, then humanity may seek to be in tune rather than in competition with the planet's other organisms and physical environment. As the WCED (1987) report argued, poor people impose excessive strains on the natural environment because of the structural demands imposed on them. Too often, 'development' has entailed control of the local environment being taken over by transnational companies and capital intensive technologies that have no long-term commitment to that environment. The environmental problems that we face are, in any case, increasingly global problems and we cannot expect others (the majority world) to act for the privileged minority in 'saving the planet' without setting a good example. The concept of majority world populations following the lead of the industrialized West, with all of the conspicuous consumption, the waste of resource, environmental pollution and exploitation that this implies is unthinkable. Primary age children should therefore be encouraged to discuss their own role, and the role of their community, in protecting the environment.

The 'problem of resources' provides the key to understanding the crisis of capitalism and ultimately to achieving world peace. It is essential that we remove the structural constraints, including the effects of debt servicing and restrictive trade barriers and agreements that currently dominate the poor majority world. If sustainable development is to be achieved then 'structural constraints' are needed, but they are needed to restrict the abusive activities of the rich minorities. In practice this will inevitably mean that the minority world populations will have to make sacrifices or, put another way, they will need to be less greedy and selfish. Many children have shown how forceful they can be in persuading their parents to give up smoking. Environmental campaigns, promoting car sharing and the use of public transport, for example, could have equivalent effects.

Balance and optimism

As Huckle (1990) suggests we should cultivate tentativeness and constructive sceptism. We should also cultivate children's capacity for constructive criticism and active environmental citizenship. We should teach in a spirit of optimism and put our faith in our children to make a better job of protecting the environment than we have. But we should also accept that we have a dual role to play as educators, not just in the privacy of our classrooms, but also in adult society. We have a responsibility as educators and as citizens to contribute towards environmental campaigns and to put into practice in our every-day lives what we profess to believe in. Perhaps this is the greatest challenge of all.

Conclusion

Despite Dobson's (1990) argument that 'no self-respecting ecologist' can accept a strong anthropocentrism that 'involves seeing the non-human world as purely a means to human ends' (Fox, 1984: 198), the dominant reality of this view is pragmatically accepted. It is essential that we avoid 'alternativism' and engage directly with this reality. Dobson recognizes that 'weak anthropocentrism' is actually a necessary feature of the human condition, and this needs to be taken further in recognition of the dominant nature of the anthropocentrism in the western world today. If we are to move beyond such narrow world-views then we must direct our critique upon the practical implications, and products of, anthropocentrism, and upon environmental pollution and technological misapplication in particular.

As Dobson has suggested, ecophilosophy has often failed to embrace the practical, as this has been seen as the role of politics. A praxis orientation would certainly be preferable. However, the philosophers may usefully map out the parameters of a future 'deep ecological' consciousness as long as they recognize what every good teacher knows: that if we are to build new understandings in children, and ultimately in society, then we must begin by identifying the existing understandings and provide new experiences and knowledge that relates to those understandings yet invites their critical reappraisal. It is to this end that this chapter has been dedicated.

Note

1 The terms 'minority world' and 'majority world' are used here as an alternative to the popular yet value loaded use of 'developed' and 'underdeveloped' or the 'developing world'. The terms also draw attention to the scale of the injustice involved in economic domination, and avoid the reification of concepts of a first/third world divide that are often grounded in notions of cultural, technical and intellectual superiority and inferiority.

References

Abraham, J., Lacey, C. and Williams, R. (eds) (1990) *Deception, Demonstration and Debate*. London: World Wildlife Fund/Kogan Page.

Bahro, R. (1982) Capitalism's global crisis. *New Statesman*, 17 December.

Bale, J. (1987) *Geography in the Primary School*. London: Routledge & Kegan Paul.

Boareman, D. and Towner, E. (1979) *Reading Ordnance Survey Maps: Some Problems of Graphicacy*. Birmingham: University of Birmingham.

Bruner, J.S. (1986) *Actual Minds, Possible Worlds*. Cambridge, Mass: Harvard University Press.

Castaneda C. (1970) *The Teachings of Don Juan: A Yacqui Way to Knowledge*. Harmondsworth: Penguin.

Department of Education and Science (DES) (1990) *Technology in the National Curriculum*. London: HMSO.

Dobson, A. (1990) *Green Political Thought*. London: HarperCollins.

Donaldson, M. (1978) *Children's Minds*. Glasgow: Fontana/Collins.

Fox, W. (1984) Deep Ecology: a new philosophy of our time?, *The Ecologist*, 14(5/6): 198.

Gillet, P. (1985) *Small is Difficult: The Pangs and Success of Small Boat Technology Transfer in South India*. Rugby: Intermediate Technology Publications.

Harding, S. (1991) *Whose Science? Whose Knowledge?: Thinking from Women's Lives*. Buckingham: Open University Press.

Hill, D. (1991) Mechanical engineering in the mediaeval Near East, *Scientific American*, 264(5): 64–70.

Huckle, J. (1990) Environmental education: teaching for a sustainable future, in B. Dufour (ed.) *The New Social Curriculum: A Guide to Cross-Curricular Issues*. Cambridge: Cambridge University Press.

Kurusa (1981) *Nowhere to Play*, translated by J. Elkin. London: Adam and Charles Black.

Layton, D. (1991) *Aspects of National Curriculum Design and Technology*. York: National Curriculum Council.

Layton, D. (1992) *Values and Design and Technology*. Design Curriculum Matters: 2, Department of Design and Technology, Loughborough University of Technology.

Levidow, L. (1987) Racism in scientific innovation, in D. Gill and L. Levidow (eds) *Anti-Racist Science Teaching*. London: Free Association Books.

Lovelock, J. (1979) *Gaia: A New Look at Life on Earth*. Oxford: Oxford University Press.

Makiya, H. and Rogers, M. (1992) *Design and Technology in the Primary School*. London: Routledge.

National Curriculum Council (NCC) (1990a) *Curriculum Guidance Four: Education for Economic Understanding*. London: HMSO.

National Curriculum Council (NCC) (1990b) *Curriculum Guidance Six: Careers Education and Guidance*. London: HMSO.

National Curriculum Council (NCC) (1990c) *Curriculum Guidance Seven: Environmental Education*. London: HMSO.

Nobel, D. (1979) *Forces of Production: A Social History of Industrial Automation*. New York: Alfred A. Knopf.

Pirsig, R. (1976) *Zen and the Art of Motorcycle Maintenance*. London: Corgi.

Rapport, A. (1980) Environmental preference, habitat selection and urban housing, *Journal of Social Issues*, 36(3) Summer: 118–34.

Redclift, M. (1984) *Development and the Environmental Crisis: Red or Green Alternatives?* London: Methuen.

Schools Council (1975) *Ethics and Education Project: Environment*. London: Longman.

Siraj-Blatchford, J. (1994) Teacher perceptions of 'good practice' and equity in primary technology education, in J. Smith (ed.) *International Conference on Design and Technology Educational Research and Curriculum Development.* Loughborough: Loughborough University of Technology.

Stirling, S. (1990) Environment, development, education – towards an holistic view, in J. Abraham, C. Lacy and R. Williams (eds) *Deception, Demonstration and Debate.* London: World Wildlife Fund/Kogan Page.

Taylor, L. and Jenkins, P. (1989) *Time to Listen: The Human Aspect in Development.* Rugby: Intermediate Technology Publications.

World Commission on Environment and Development (WCED) (1987) *Our Common Future.* Oxford: Oxford University Press.

Useful sources

Brown, L. (1988) *State of the World.* London: W.W. Norton.

Budgett-Meakin, C. (ed.) (1992) *Make the Future Work: Appropriate Technology, A Teachers' Guide.* London: Longman.

Capra, F. (1982) *The Turning Point: Science, Society and the Rising Culture.* London: Wildwood House.

Carson, R. (1963) *Silent Spring.* London: Hamish Hamilton.

Gorz, A. (1982) *Farewell to the Working Class: An Essay on Post-industrial Socialism.* London: Pluto Press.

Grieg, S., Pike, G. and Selby, D. (eds) (1987) *Earthrights: Education as if the Planet Really Mattered.* London: World Wildlife Fund/Kogan Page.

Visram, R. (1994) British history: whose history? black perspectives on British history, in H. Bourdillon (ed.) *Teaching History.* London: Routledge in association with the Open University.

9

JOHN BENNETT,
BALBIR KAUR SOHAL and
JANICE WALE

Health education in
the primary school:
back to basics?

Editors' introduction

In 1993 the Conservative government under John Major's
leadership launched an ill-fated 'back-to-basics' campaign.
One of the main planks of this campaign was a reassertion
of alleged traditional family values, and much of the rhetoric
had a distinctly American flavour. Among other things the
campaign emphasized the need for children to be brought up
in homes with two heterosexual parents, who committed
themselves to staying together until their children were
adults, regardless of family discord. The Conservatives
directly challenged the growing tolerance of alternative
family structures and among those that came under their
onslaught were single-parent families. Ironically, the
campaign floundered as politicians themselves were shown by
the media to be unable to live according to their own
rhetoric. In this chapter John Bennett, Balbir Kaur Sohal and
Janice Wale argue that in spite of some families facing
domestic discord and economic hardship, in education we
must begin with the experiences of family life that children
bring into school with them. Teacher's must work with the
families in a respectful way so that children are not alienated
and are able to grow to make their own reasoned and
rational decisions for their future lives. The authors argue
that family life education is an important vehicle for teaching

about the various components of health education and
children's rights, and that through this children can learn to
exercise their own rights and begin to make decisions for
themselves.

Introduction

The publication of *Curriculum Guidance Five: Health Education* (CG5) by
the National Curriculum Council (NCC 1990a) clearly outlined for the first
time the breadth of concern covered by health education by breaking it
down into nine discrete components. Previously, health educational provision had been determined as more of a reactive response to contemporary
issues and concerns. Provision of this kind dated from the early days of state
education when 'physical training' and 'hygiene' were taught as a response
to the poor state of public health amongst the working classes, right up to
the present day when similar 'health of the nation' provision has targeted
teenage pregnancies and focuses on sex education in schools. Health education, in its various forms, has thus been an integral part of the whole curriculum for some considerable time.

For many schools 'health education' has meant a general concern with
the physical well-being of pupils, but CG5 (NCC 1990a) provides a broader
rationale that defines 'health' in the wider context of 'mental' and 'social'
well-being. The importance of health education has been emphasized between 1986 and 1993 when Grants for Education and Training (GEST)
as well as Education Support Grants (ESGs) were made available to fund
health education coordinators and provide training in preventive health
education issues. Although these posts were initially concerned with drug
misuse, from 1990 the brief was extended to the more general health education to help implement the nine components defined by CG5.

These nine components are: substance use and misuse, sex education,
family life education, health related exercise, food and nutrition, personal
hygiene, the environment and safety and psychological health. The guidance emphasises that although health education is not an additional subject,
it is one of the cross-curricular themes as identified in NCC *Circular
Number Six*:

> It is not an additional subject. Many of the elements of health educa-
> tion can be taught through the subjects of the National Curriculum
> and other timetabled provisions, in addition to being promoted
> through the wider aspects of school life.
>
> (NCC 1989)

Family life education or education for life?

The rest of this chapter is broken into the component parts outlined within CG5 (NCC 1990a). However, when we started to write this chapter we were concerned that the context for health education should be firmly anchored within the family and that equality issues should permeate the whole approach. We felt that 'family life' should be more than just one of the components as education for health begins in the home where patterns of behaviour and attitudes influence health for good or ill throughout life and will be well established before the child is 5 (HMSO 1986). In each of the other components we have therefore tried to illustrate the issues that are related to the family and 'family life'.

We emphasize throughout the chapter our concern at the damage being done to the psychological health of children by the economic inequalities facing them from birth. These are further compounded by other forms of deprivation and oppression such as homophobia, sexism, racism and disability. Our examples take up these issues as we feel that they are too important to ignore. We firmly believe that time should be made to discuss and debate the issues with children. We also feel that throughout all health education programmes the emphasis should be upon the importance of teaching those life skills that will enable children not only to understand the influences and constraints that act upon their lives but also to empower them to make informed choices and to equip them to take control over their lives.

The family life component

Most primary schools recognize the critical role the family plays within the life of the child, however, very few so far actually explore the issues relating to living within a family or help children distinguish myths and stereotypes from reality, as required as one of the aims in *Curriculum Guidance Eight: Citizenship* (CG8) (NCC 1990b).

The family life component is concerned with the child's role within the family and considers different types of family groupings, roles within families, and the rituals associated with birth, marriage and death. At first sight the component may appear uncontroversial but with the changing face of 'the family' with, for example, parents opting not to marry, conflict is arising. In 1988, 29.9 per cent of births to people under 20 were to unmarried couples (HMSO 1991). Various politicians and others have wished to maintain the teaching of what they see as 'traditional family structures' and would criticize those who do not agree with what they perceive as an 'ideal' model. This issue is represented in the Department for Education (DFE) Circular 5/94 in the section 'A moral framework for sex education':

Pupils should accordingly be encouraged to appreciate the values of stable family life, marriage and the responsibilities of parenthood. They should be helped to consider the importance of self esteem, dignity, respect for themselves and others, acceptance of responsibility, sensitivity towards the needs and views of others, loyalty and fidelity.

Teachers need to acknowledge that many children come from backgrounds that do not reflect such values or experiences. Sensitivity is therefore needed to avoid giving hurt and offence to them and their families: and to allow such children to feel a sense of worth. But teachers should also help pupils, whatever their circumstances to raise their sights.

(DFE 1994: 6)

This, by implication, sets the worth of a particular family grouping higher or lower on a scale of values imposed by government.

We have been concerned at the recent attacks on the family taking place in government and the media and the resultant damage that this may be doing to those pupils who are being promoted as issuing from 'deviant' family systems. The family is being seen as the institution which is to blame for many of society's ills, and it is the institution which is charged with the responsibility of putting those ills right (Development Education Centre (DEC) 1991). As Rosalind Coward has said, with the Bulger case, the rising crime rate amongst younger children and deteriorating behaviour patterns within schools, there are very few who have not wondered whether the huge changes in family patterns, in education and in criminal activity, all with children at their centre, have not delivered up a 'crisis of childhood' (Coward 1994). We feel that these issues need to be debated within education and in partnership with children, parents and/or carers. Until this happens many of the detrimental factors that are affecting the psychological well-being of children will remain. If a child's family is presented as deviant, in the child's eyes there is something wrong with them, and unless they are given the chance to articulate and discuss their feelings they will internalize the oppression, becoming unhappy and alienated from the rest of society. For some the *cycle of deviance* will begin with behavioural patterns that challenge those they are unable to relate to.

One of the authors of this chapter experienced this feeling of 'difference' throughout her own childhood years:

As the eldest of six children I was acutely aware that this was something not to be proud of. Everyone around, including teachers, made me feel uncomfortable, treating the fact as something deviant. Their attitude affected the way I thought about my family – it affected my emotional and psychological well-being and I grew up thinking

there was something wrong with my father and mother because they
had had so many children.

Children who come from family groupings that differ from the supposed
norm such as those from parents who are divorced or those who may have
a single mother, or parents who are lesbian or gay or disabled, may also
experience this feeling of being different and of their family as deviant.
Children from black and ethnic minority families may also be vulnerable
as they are constantly bombarded with white ethnic majority family images
as the norm.

Parents in any 'type' of family might have problems and we need to
remind ourselves that 'family life' for a significant number of children is not
the loving, caring institution that the media and most teachers imply. There
are children who are coming to our classrooms hungry, unwashed, ill and
physically and emotionally abused. Some might see abuse of their mothers,
while others see their parents stressed and unable to cope with caring for
their children. The list of family problems is endless. In one class a child
whose mother and father were in prison informed their teacher that his
uncle had raped his own two year-old daughter. Another child masturbated
her mother's 'clients' while they waited. Another came to school in the depth
of winter in a T-shirt; his mother did not have the parenting skills needed
or the finance to support her family. He, along with his sisters and brothers,
were continually in and out of 'care'. There were other children in this class
with a range of family 'problems'. The children were all 6 years of age. If
we fail to acknowledge that some families are not the loving caring groups
shown on the television or in books, then children are not only being dam-
aged by their families but also by education which is reinforcing the mytho-
logy. The child will end up feeling that their family is the only 'deviant' one.
It is quite clear that some families need a great deal of help and support
to care for their children.

We would argue that inequality issues should be at the forefront of
teachers' minds when they are planning as they impact on the health of rich
and poor alike. While the government, through the Health Department,
reacts to the 'flavour of the month' media campaign, vacillating with funding between anti-drug campaigns, HIV/Aids education and teenage preg-
nancy issues, the youngest children in our schools are also living the daily
reality of inequality and injustice which strikes at the heart of any health
education programme.

Wilkinson has found that inequality is the single most damaging factor
to the health of the nation (Donnison 1994). However young they are,
children pick up the hidden messages from the adults around them and if
they are not allowed the space to articulate their concerns and fears then
we as educationalists are failing. As teachers we must acknowledge that

health education is not about imparting knowledge but about acknowledging that children need to be taught the skills to enable them to deal with the world in which they live; they need to explore fundamental questions such as:

- why there is inequality;
- why there is poverty;
- why there is unemployment;
- why people are homeless;
- why there is so much injustice;
- why people die of malnutrition while others live in opulence;
- why some families have fewer physical or emotional resources to enable them to deal with problems which could face any family.

Children need to understand the economics that exclude and exploit increasing numbers of people, destroy human relationships and blight lives. They need to understand that they are social animals, that there *is* such a thing as 'society' (Donnison 1994), and that what happens in 'society' affects all our health and our psychological well-being. Only if children are given the time and skills to assess critically, to discuss complex dilemmas, can they begin to rehearse their roles as responsible adults and to make the informed choices required of them (Carrington and Troyna 1988).

Many primary school teachers do now teach about the inequalities related to sexism and racism but very little is done on economic deprivation except sometimes as part of a project relating to what are euphemistically, and in recent years quite incorrectly termed 'economically developing countries'. Teachers are often more comfortable debating these issues if they are removed from the immediate experiences of their pupils. Many feel that primary school children are too young to be discussing controversial issues and we often hear them suggest that it 'might make it worse by talking about this'. This protective attitude leads teachers to make judgements about what constitutes 'normal' values and to underestimate the pupils' existing experience and awareness of the issues involved.

Topics on 'the family' are actually included in nearly every primary school as the subject is rarely seen as controversial. We have even witnessed topics focused on 'my mum' or 'my dad'. When playing in the playhouse most children are engaged in exploring and reaffirming family roles and responsibilities and it is here that some teachers now try to encourage non-stereotypical gender role-play. They talk about the roles with the children and allow them to read stories and use resources that emphasize the various roles that people in families may have (Coventry Education Department 1993a).

While some teachers are now addressing the question 'what is a family?', using resources such as that produced by the Birmingham Development

Education Centre (DEC) (1990) which ensure that the range of family structures and forms are represented, there are still many who present 'the family' as the nuclear structure perpetuated by the reading schemes of the past. That is, of a working father, a mother at home with two children, a boy and a girl and maybe a dog. We were reminded of how pervasive this image still is when a couple we know gave birth to twins, a girl and a boy. This was greeted by almost everyone as 'wonderful – an instant family'. The same was not said to parents who had one child or even when the twins were of the same sex. Teachers are bringing to 'family life' education their own attitudes and values which are based on their own socialization processes that have included and still include those images that present outdated models of the 'normal' family. Teachers need to be aware of the messages we give to those children who are not part of this supposed 'ideal' and invariably white, heterosexual and non-disabled family.

Disability is an area that is rarely addressed within the mainstream classroom. A few teachers may use the resources of the visually impaired units or invite in a non-sighted person with their guide-dog but the issues for family life are rarely addressed. Again we need to think carefully about the messages and harm this may be doing not only to disabled children themselves but also to children who may have a parent or carer who is disabled as well as non-disabled children. These children are already living in a world that rarely acknowledges the existence of disabled people. A world where they or their family is invisible and gives the message that they are unimportant and there is something wrong with them. Our segregated schooling system only serves to reinforce these messages.

The family life component suggests that children be involved in activities relating to birth, marriage and death but this is always in the context of non-disabled images, as too is the work done in the science curriculum. Richard Reiser and Micheline Mason debate these issues for education in their book *Disability, Equality In The Classroom: A Human Rights Issue* (1990) and suggest activities for the classroom. One of these involves using a 'cartoon' of people at the birth of a new baby and asks 'why are the people looking sad?'

To raise issues relating to disability Coventry City Council ran a 'Disability Awareness Week' and all schools were given a pack of materials for use in the classroom. The cartoon mentioned above was included in the material and we found children debating the issues with a sensitivity and foresight that may often be lacking in adults. For the nursery and early years classes we gave a copy of *Ruby* by Maggie Glen (1992) which proved a successful way of introducing issues relating to impairment and 'difference'. Children were asked to say in what ways *Ruby* was special (Coventry Education Department 1993b).

As previously stated, some teachers are looking at the different family structures and others are acknowledging the various cultural and ethnic groupings within society. For example some schools are asking their South Asian parents to demonstrate the art of baby massage not only to the children but also to their parent groups. The South Asian parents are then able to talk about child-rearing practices relating to their particular culture. There are, however, still many who do *not* tackle the issues of racism and racial harassment. This is despite the devastating fact that it has actually led to 'murder in the playground' (Macdonald *et al.* 1989). Racist behaviour and harassment affects not only the children in our schools but their families as well. Many parents may find it difficult to find employment because of racist attitudes and many black people can be found on low incomes and living in poor housing.

There is not the space here to debate the issues fully but the psychological and physical damage that this may be doing to black and white children is well documented and is central to the debate within the Burnage Report (Macdonald *et al.* 1989). Iram Siraj-Blatchford has discussed the major issues to be considered in Chapter 4 of this book. Parents find it difficult to place faith in an education system where their children continue to be abused and where, when they report their concerns, they are told by the child's teacher, 'you are over reacting, being called chocolate drop is no different to being called lanky legs' (an interaction reported to one of the authors by a teacher). We would argue that all forms of abuse are wrong and should be dealt with by school staff as well as other appropriate support agencies. However, as a child explained to his year 4 class: 'when they call me "Paki" it not only hurts me, but it's hurting all my family and all Asians everywhere'. This child was allowed to discuss his feeling because his teacher felt that the issues were too important to ignore (Coventry Education Department 1993a: 94).

In recent months we have witnessed what has amounted to a government attack on single/lone parents. These families, due to death, divorce, separation, migration and births to women without long-term partners are mainly headed by women. Single-parent families represent one of the most vulnerable forms of family, and one of the easiest targets for discrimination (Watterson 1994). We must ensure that the children from these family structures who are trying to make sense of the messages they are being given are enabled to see that their family is not deviant. They must also be given space to discuss any concerns they have in dealing with the images being given them from politicians and the media.

As part of their topic on 'My Family' a nursery class drew pictures. When Laura drew her family some of the children in the class asked 'where is your daddy?' Laura quite confidently discussed the fact that 'he doesn't live with us any more and I can't see him very often because of the CSA'. This child may not understand the intricacies of the Child Support Agency but she has understood its effect on herself and the rest of her family. She is being helped by her teacher who values all family structures and shows this through the stories, pictures and language she uses to introduce the topic. At the age of 4 Laura may not be able to debate the issues but her elder brother *is* able to and teachers need to be aware that these issues can and do relate to their pupils. Some of these children were also being taken on demonstrations against the Child Support Agency and this was also an experience that should not have been ignored.

The above issues, experiences and curriculum work are obviously not all inclusive and form only the 'tip of the iceberg' where family life education is concerned but we would like to move on to discuss issues relating to the other eight components included in the CG5 (1990a). In recent years, 'sex education' and 'substance use and misuse' have been a particular concern of parents and the Government and for this reason we articulate below the requirements and issues for these key components in more detail than those relating to the other six. This is not meant to imply that we feel the issues relating to those six components are of any less importance.

Sex education

Sex education, unlike family life, has always been a controversial issue and the question of how it should be presented in schools is still an ongoing debate. There are some who still argue that sex education encourages promiscuity, early exploration and unwanted teenage pregnancies. This argument is, however, not borne out by the research evidence (Jones 1986). In fact research suggests that knowledge about sex-related issues does not increase young people's sexual activities but instead leads to a more responsible and informed behaviour.

The main legislative change that has taken place in this area for primary schools is that relating to the parent's right to withdraw their child from the sex education lesson. Previously parents had to apply to the governing body for the right to withdraw and the final decision rested with the governors of the school. The 1993 Education Act, Section 241 (DFE 1993) now gives parents an automatic right to withdraw their child from sex education, however, the situation remains complicated as DFE Circular 5/94 states:

> The Secretary of State intends that there should continue to be a requirement for pupils at Key Stages 1 and 2 to be taught about human reproduction and development. As for all topics which are specified in the National Curriculum, parents are not entitled to withdraw their children from this teaching.

> (DFE 1994: 8)

In June 1994 a letter was sent from the DFE which attempted to clarify the position by stating that science teaching should relate to the biological 'facts' and that human sexual behaviour and issues such as HIV and AIDS and other sexually transmitted diseases should form part of a separate sex education syllabus. Although the letter was intended to clarify the position at Key Stage Three it applies equally to primary schools.

It is expected that very few parents will wish to exercise their right to withdraw as it has been found that many parents are very supportive and wish schools to teach sex education. Allen (1987) found that 96 per cent of parents and 95 per cent of children wanted schools to provide sex education. These views may also be taken to include parents from the many different religious and ethnic groups as long as sex education is presented in the context of loving, heterosexual relationships and for the purpose of procreation (Thomson 1993). Although there may be distinct sects within different faith groups who object to all sex education, all the major religions represented in Britain are supportive as long as their views are respected. Issues such as HIV, sexuality and contraception are more usually covered at secondary school but if a primary aged child asks a question a simple answer might be the most appropriate response. This very common eventuality should be discussed by all staff and appropriate guidance included in the school's policy.

Using CG5 (NCC 1990a) as a framework at Key stage One, the only area that teachers may find difficult is the naming of the body parts including the reproductive organs. This is intended to give a more serious approach to the subject rather than the use of familiar or familial names which are numerous. At a recent training session with parents in a Coventry school for example, the penis was referred to as a 'maggot' and a 'caterpillar'. Such terminology is obviously confusing and some children are likely to be developing quite strange notions about their body parts. The use of the proper terminology within the classroom helps children get over the 'giggle' factor.

At Key Stage Two children are required to understand the physical, emotional and social changes that take place at puberty. They are also required to know the basic biology of human reproduction and understand the physical skills necessary for parenting. Using the suggestions outlined in CG5 (NCC 1990a) should enable primary schools to provide sex education that meets the needs of the children, has parents' support and that teachers feel comfortable delivering.

One area that is rarely talked about with pupils at primary or secondary level is sexual harassment and the power relationship between boys and girls. The images of masculinity based on aggression and power are often played out in the sexual relationships with young men treating young women as sex objects rather than in building caring relationships (Lees 1986, 1993). Many popular images of what constitutes female and male behaviour are still extremely sexist. Boys and girls who do not conform to popular images of what passes for femininity and masculinity can suffer from harassment and abuse from the early years. As one year four boy has told us: 'I've been called wimp, poof, fairy, or gay every day at school because I don't like football and I like to play with the girls'. The school did nothing for him. If he complained the staff would often say 'ignore it' or, what was worse, 'call them names back'. The psychological damage being done to this child was horrendous and until we began the work on harassment and bullying he had never been offered an opportunity to dis-cuss these very important issues, not only about the harassment but also about the images of masculinity. Through introducing reading material and resources that raised these issues we were able to assure this young boy that masculinity did not depend on being macho and aggressive. One of the activities involved talking about the roles of mothers and fathers and exploring whether they felt that boys and girls are different. The class then made a poster with the title 'He May Be A Father One Day' to illustrate that boys and men could be sensitive and caring and have a nurturing role as fathers. Most people agree that relationship education is of vital impor-tance whatever the age of the child. By discussing the issues in an appropriate way at primary school we may help to alleviate some of the problems encountered by teenagers.

Many people feel that sexual harassment is not an issue for primary schools but if we look around we will see that it is very prevalent. One teacher in Coventry was so concerned at the acceptance of behaviours that constituted sexual harassment in her reception class (the lifting of skirts, the pulling down of trousers) as 'just a joke' and the use of the term 'slag' whenever there was an argument that she decided to teach assertiveness skills to the girls (Coventry Education Department 1993a). She found that the girls were quite distressed at what had been taking place but did not have the necessary skills to deal with the situations without resorting to fighting. In confronting the perpetrators and telling them how they felt about their behaviour the girls were helped and the boys were disconcerted to find themselves being challenged in a calm, direct and honest, non-violent way.

Substance use and abuse

The component 'substance use and misuse' emphasizes how there is more to these issues than reflected in the simplistic title 'drugs'. For many people 'drugs' simply means a concern with illegal substances and for many pri-mary schools there is a feeling that this was not an issue for them. This is certainly not true of all primary schools. It was the concern shown by primary teachers in the Wirral that led to the publication of *Health Education – Drugs and the Primary School Child* by The Advisory Council for Alcohol and Drug Education (TACADE) (Rees 1988). In general health terms there are also concerns about legal drugs such as alcohol and tobacco which often directly affect the lives of adults and children. For most of our pupils these are far more likely to lead to ill health or even death than illegal substances. It is also significant that the Health Education Authority's (HEA) (1992) study of young people's life styles found a very strong correlation between teenage smoking and illegal drug use. In fact, 54 per cent of the smokers had used, or were using, illegal drugs compared to only 2 per cent of the non-smokers.

Drug education must take place in the primary school if it is to have any impact on the lives of young people as they come into contact with situations where they may be offered drugs. The Smoking Education for Teenagers Project based at Bristol and Exeter Universities found that research based on 10,599 young people produced the following results:

- 3 per cent of boys and 2 per cent of girls claimed to have tried their first cigarette by the age of five,
- 10 per cent of boys and 7 per cent of girls claimed to have tried their first cigarette by the first year of junior school,
- 43 per cent of boys and 31 per cent of girls claimed to have tried their first cigarette by the age of eleven.

(taken from HEA 1987)

Substance use and misuse is therefore an issue for all primary schools and appropriate methodologies need to be explored. These should not include the 'shock/horror' or 'just say no' approaches as these have both failed. The 'shock/horror' might scare children in the short term but has no lasting impact for a variety of reasons. Children often see or hear about drug taking and they see that the results were not as dire or immediate as they had been led to believe. They are then encouraged to try it for themselves as their friends have not come to any particular harm. The 'just say no' approach is far to simplistic. How many teachers or parents say no to things that they know are not good for them such as alcohol, cigarettes, fatty food and sweets? Knowledge does not always change behaviour patterns. *Every* smoker in Britain knows that it is damaging their health, but a significant minority of adults still choose to smoke.

The approaches that do appear to have some effect are the development of personal life skills that are not exclusive to health education, and these skills form the basis of good educational practice. The skills include self-awareness, decision making, empathy, communication and assertiveness

which all combine to build confident, articulate people able to make thoughtful choices. These approaches can be used with children of all ages and an
excellent example can be found in *Learning To Be Strong: Developing
Assertiveness with Young Children* which outlines the work of the staff with
nursery children at Pen Green Family Centre in Corby (Pen Green Family
Centre 1990). Other resources that we have found very successful are *The
Whole Child* which introduces the United Nations Convention's Rights of
the Child 8–13: this resource particularly concentrates on the Participation
Articles and covers many activities to encourage children to participate in
their own learning (Save the Children and UNICEF 1990).

The six other components, safety, health related exercise, food and nutrition, personal hygiene, the environment and psychological health identified
in CG5 (NCC 1990a) all provide guidance that is relevant to 'family life'
education as well as being health elements in their own right. Due to the
restrictions on space we cannot engage with all of these but we will outline
those that we feel are particularly pertinent to issues of inequality.

Health related exercise

Research conducted by Armstrong (1989) has found that although the
majority of children in his study were fit they were not as active as they
would need to be to maintain a healthy life. The primary years are important as they set down the foundation for the latter years and opportunities
should be sought to offer activities that will improve general health. This
may include extra-curricular activities and Armstrong stresses the need to
encourage family involvement. Again, this will be easier for some groups
of pupils than others but a whole school policy should outline ways to
involve parents who may be particularly vulnerable themselves.

Food and nutrition

Teachers need to be careful not to impose values about good or bad food.
Children's choice of food may be constrained by a variety of factors such as
culture and economics. They may receive messages about food and diet that
conflict with their home background. Advertisements give false images of
women and men with so-called perfect bodies which we should all be aim-
ing for otherwise we will not be normal, or men and women as 'special';
for example, the mother in the special K advertisement (1994). Some
children take on these messages and some even ask their overweight parents
not to go to school events – such experiences are heartbreaking for all concerned. Work on nutrition should involve debate on media images as well

as the economic forces that control our choice of food. *We Are What We Eat, but Who Controls Our Choice?* (UNICEF 1990) is an excellent resource to use when raising these issues.

Personal hygiene

This is usually regarded as a non-controversial component but again cultural and economic factors may affect a family's attitude to hygiene or limit the extent to which they can achieve what they see as desirable. For instance, the very high standards of Islamic conventions regarding personal hygiene should be ones that teachers familiarize themselves with. Prayer is always preceded by washing and some practising Muslims, for example, are expected to use only their right hand in eating as the use of the left is seen as unclean. It should not be assumed, however, that the experiences and practices of *all* Islamic families and children are the same. Some families will object to communal showers especially for their daughters for doctrinal reasons. Many other children find the experience of communal showering traumatic and schools should consider their policies carefully in the light of children's rights legislation and principles.

The environment

Environmental aspects of health education are linked to issues such as pollution and respect for the local environment. Little is mentioned of the damaging effects to health of poor housing or high-rise flats which may be a major issue for many children in schools. Environmental issues are not value free and while a new factory might cause pollution it may also bring much needed jobs which may mean healthier life styles for a considerable number of people. Through debating issues such as these children begin to see that these issues are complex and require careful deliberation.

Safety

The safety component is concerned with all aspects from the safe environment and avoiding dangers from roads to personal safety. Again this involves families whose attitudes as to what is 'safe' will be shaped by their own environment, culture and experiences. Keeping safe from abuse is an area now covered in most schools and the personal skills needed to be taught are usefully outlined in *Learning To Be Strong* (Pen Green Family Centre 1990) and other literature on child protection.

Psychological health

The final component within the health education guidelines is psychological health which we feel has been the main thrust of this chapter. We have tried to demonstrate that family and national health is not just about physical well-being but also about psychological well-being. We have attempted to point out how inequality and division in society brings with it damage to the health of many people. There is a need to raise issues that relate to the psychological well-being of people and to debate these with pupils.

Conclusion

With the changes that have taken place in education over the past few years the reality facing education is that many teachers feel demoralized, with less energy and enthusiasm. Reports from the National Union of Teachers (NUT 1989) have found that these changes have affected the health of teachers as the levels of stress have risen. Many teachers feel overwhelmed by the demands of the National Curriculum and feel there is little time to meet the real needs of pupils that health education and the other themes and dimensions demand. The Thomas Report (ILEA 1985) found that when classroom practice consists mainly of teaching basic skills and knowledge, and when the assessment of achievement dominates, there is little opportunity for the introduction of controversial issues. However, pupils *are* receiving very confusing messages from society and if schools never engage with pupils about these messages then they may feel alienated from the whole schooling process. The new National Curriculum that has resulted from the Dearing Report (1994) is freeing up some time that should enable teachers to reassess their approach and enable them to help children negotiate meanings to the complex and divided society that we live in and to understand the influences and constraints on their lives. Psychological health means giving pupils a positive self-esteem and motivation which means teaching the attitudes, values and the life skills that will enable children to enter the 21st century as happy, healthy, confident and capable citizens.

References

Allen, I. (1987) *Education in Sex and Personal Relationships*. London: Policy Studies Institute.
Armstrong, N. (1989) Children are fit but not active. *Health Education Journal*, 7(2): 28.
Carrington, B. and Troyna, B. (eds) (1988) *Children and Controversial Issues:*

Strategies for the Early and Middle Years of Schooling. Lewes: Falmer Press.

Coventry Education Department (1993a) *Equality of Opportunity in the Classroom.* Coventry: Coventry Education Department.

Coventry Education Department (1993b) *Disability Awareness Week Teacher Pack.* Coventry: Coventry Education Department.

Coward, R. (1994) Even Will Shakespeare was a lousy dad. *The Observer Review,* 31 July.

Dearing, Sir R. (1994) *The National Curriculum and its Assessment* (the Dearing Report). London: National Curriculum Council.

Department for Education (DFE) (1994) Circular 5/94 – *Sex Education.* London: HMSO.

Department for Education (DFE) (1993) *Education Act 1993.* London: HMSO.

Development Education Centre (DEC) (1990) *What is a Family?* Birmingham (Selly Oak): DEC.

Development Education Centre (DEC) (1991) *Values Cultures and Kids and Resources for Teaching about Family Education.* Cheltenham: Stanley Thornes.

Donnison, D. (1994) Riches to die for. The *Guardian,* 27 July.

Glen, M. (1992) *Ruby.* London: Hutchinson.

Health Education Authority (HEA) (1987) *Smoking and Me.* London: Health Education Authority.

Health Education Authority (HEA) (1992) *Young People's Lifestyles.* London: Health Education Authority.

HMSO (1986) *Curriculum Matters Six – Health Education from 5–16.* London: HMSO.

HMSO (1991) *Social Trends 21.* London: HMSO.

Inner London Education Authority (ILEA) (1985) *Improving Primary Schools* (the Thomas Report). London: ILEA.

Jones, E.F. (1986) *Teenage Pregnancies in Industrial Countries.* Allan Gutterman Institute New Haven CT: Yale University Press.

Lees, S. (1986) *Losing Out.* London: Heinemann.

Lees, S. (1993) *Sugar and Spice: Sexuality and Adolescent Girls.* London: Penguin.

Macdonald, I., Bhavnani, R., Khan, L. and John, G. (1989) *Murder in The Playground* (the Burnage Report). London: Longsight Press.

National Curriculum Council (NCC) (1989) *The National Curriculum and Whole Curriculum Planning – Circular Number Six.* York: NCC.

National Curriculum Council (NCC) (1990a) *Curriculum Guidance Five: Health Education.* York: NCC.

National Curriculum Council (NCC) (1990b) *Curriculum Guidance Eight: Citizenship.* York: NCC.

National Union of Teachers (1989) *Teachers and Schools: A Study of Organisational Health and Stress.* London: National Union of Teachers.

Pen Green Family Centre (1990) *Learning To Be Strong: Developing Assertiveness with Young Children.* Cheshire: Changing Perspectives Ltd. (obtainable from Penn Green Family Centre, Corby, Northants).

Rees, S. (1988) *Health Education – Drugs and the Primary School Child*. Salford: TACADE/Health Education Council.

Reiser, R. and Mason, M. (1990) *Disability, Equality In the Classroom: A Human Rights Issue*. London: London Education Authority.

Save the Children and UNICEF (UK) (1990) *The Whole Child: The Participation Articles*. Oxford: Oxford DEC.

Thomson, R. (ed.) (1993) *Religion, Ethnicity and Sex Education: Exploring the Issues*. London: National Children's Bureau.

UNICEF (1990) *We Are What We Eat, but Who Controls Our Choice?* London: UNICEF.

Watterson, J. (1994) Families: is there a fitting image? *Common Cause* (Action Aid Newsletter) January–March.

10

PETER LANG

The place of PSE in the primary school

Editors' introduction

In the following pages Peter Lang considers
the nature of personal and social education (PSE) in
primary schools, Peter offers practical suggestions for
developing PSE at policy, pedagogic and curriculum
levels and argues forcibly for overarching PSE
policies that will inform future developments across
the whole curriculum. He also provides further
examples of the use of 'circle time' with 4 to 9 year-
olds and argues that both planned provision and
spontaneous responses are essential qualities. Peter
provides a critical account of the development of the
subject and argues that the National Curriculum
Council's (NCC) cross-curriculum guidance has led
to confusion. The emphasis upon the separate
themes has served to distract attention from the need
to define overarching PSE policies that encourage
children to reflect upon their experiences,
collaboratively seek explanations and develop
initiative, responsibility and mature relationships.

Citing research evidence, Peter argues that the
quality of current provision varies widely and that
counter-productive disciplinary practices such as
'public humiliation' are still practised in some schools.

Many of the contributions to this volume have emphasized the need for schools to undertake a fundamental re-evaluation of who and what education is really for. For Peter, the major challenge for schools is the self-critical and collaborative identification of the values that are reflected in their fundamental aims. These need to be reviewed in the light of a thorough examination and analysis of 'needs'. In all of this the needs of the child should be central, but as Anne Sinclair Taylor and Debra Costley have suggested in their chapter on 'special needs' (Chapter 3), a commitment by staff to pupils' personal and social education really pays off in encouraging wider participation and school effectiveness.

Introduction: the nature of personal and social education

Last year I was working with a class of 7, 8 and 9 year-olds in a first school. I spent an hour a week with them and this involved all of us working in a circle. This approach, 'circle time' will be described later in the chapter. One method I used involved animal puppets. The puppets were about to go to the animal school and the circle were encouraged to tell them of the sort of problems they might encounter and what they might do about them, and in this way the class actually started to talk through some of their own problems and to think of strategies for handling them. I owe the idea for this approach to Jenny Mosley whom I observed using the technique. The following week when I joined the class for our circle work I found that many of the children had brought their own stuffed animals. They had spontaneously decided that my puppets would feel more comfortable and less threatened talking to them. At the end of the year we were using the circle to consider how those going up to the middle school felt. In the circle a special object was passed round and the children could only talk when they had the object. Each child who was moving on had a turn with the object and talked of how excited they were and how much they were looking forward to things. When everyone had finished I took the object and asked 'is there anything you are not looking forward to?' A boy took the object and said 'yes I am really going to miss Miss Spencer'. This was their excellent young teacher. After this a flood of feelings were expressed/ released about the sense of loss they had at leaving Miss Spencer.

The point about these two examples is that while they were both spontaneous, the spontaneity was possible because of the conscious and planned process involved. A range of skills and qualities that might normally be associated with Personal and Social Education (PSE) had been encouraged. The examples actually highlight a key feature of PSE; that to be effective it must involve both planning and spontaneity. Of course the approach I have described also developed skills that related to the pupils' effectiveness as learners. Another example of this is the circle work I have undertaken in the same school with the reception classes. Here an important developmental goal is to promote an understanding of how others in the circle feel (simple empathy), and this is partly achieved through developing the pupils' questioning skills, which is in itself an important learning objective for these classes.

Above I have described as PSE a situation were everyone is equally in control, where one can talk when one has the object, and everyone has the same right to talk and the same responsibility to listen. Equally in some cases assemblies where children are talked to, videos followed by teacher led discussion, or classes working at individual worksheet are also described as PSE. Thus, PSE potentially embraces a wide range of approaches. Equally, when definitions of PSE are offered they tend to be broad and allow for considerable variation in interpretation. They can range from the short and idealistic:

> For present purposes we define this simply as all learning experiences which give pupils a developing sense of their own abilities and of their rights and responsibilities as contributing members of the school and of the wider community in which they live.
>
> (Galloway 1990: 6)

To the rather more developed and specific:

> In this paper personal and social education refers to those aspects of a schools thinking, planning, teaching and organisation explicitly designed to promote the personal and social development of pupils. It does not follow that arrangements should necessarily include timetabled courses specifically concerned with personal and social education. Personal and social education is concerned with qualities and attitudes, knowledge and understanding, and abilities and skills in relation to oneself and others, social responsibilities and morality. It helps pupils to be considerate and enterprising in the present, while it prepares them for an informed and active involvement in family, social, economic and civic life. It plays an important part in bringing relevance, breadth and balance to the curriculum.
>
> (DES 1989: 1)

Definitions of this kind do give a general feeling of the nature of PSE, and indeed this is all they set out to do, but they offer little help in relation to two important elements of PSE. How should specific aims and objectives be developed and how can policies be developed which transform these aims and objectives into practice? It is these issues that are at the centre of this chapter, which having considered the current situation will go on to suggest an approach which the writer believes will develop both appropriate and effective PSE within individual schools. First, however, the nature of PSE will be considered further.

Defining PSE

PSE is an explicit process which implies planning, conscious action and reflection. The aim is to effect the personal and social development of pupils in ways that are seen as beneficial, and there is some intentionality involved. It is in relation to the question of what constitutes 'beneficial' that one of the major problems of PSE exists. This problem has already been identified by Galloway:

> The problem is that individuals or groups who influence the curriculum conceptualise the aims of personal and social education in different ways. A DES/HMI report, for example, talks about pupils forming 'an acceptable set of personal values' (p. 2). They do not, because they could not, define what personal values are 'acceptable'. The reason is that acceptability is determined by the prevailing beliefs, and the values associated with beliefs, within particular communities.
>
> (Galloway 1990: 6)

It is because of the variation in views of what is beneficial that it is not possible to provide highly specific definitions. In the light of this it should be noted that the view of PSE being presented here, though based on widely held views, remains at least in part a particular perspective, and that the possibility of other interpretations exists. An important aspect of the concern of PSE relates to the attitudes, feelings, beliefs and emotions of pupils, and of course of teachers. Pupil self-esteem can be seen as one of the specific focuses of this concern. A further important aspect goes beyond the individual pupil and concerns the quality of their relationship with others. Thus, interpersonal relationships and social skills are a central concern. Responsibility and autonomy can be seen as another aspect of PSE; the ability to act in an autonomous way, to be assertive and take responsibility for one's actions and oneself, and this extends to the degree to which a pupil can be brought to take responsibility for their own learning. PSE certainly involves work of a proactive nature, aimed at equipping pupils to handle problems such as bullying, abuse, racism, sexism or conflict in general.

More detailed interpretations of PSE should relate to the situation of the particular school concerned. Things which might be taken into account are the school's catchment area, the needs of its pupils, the attitudes, strengths and weaknesses of its staff and what its priorities are at that time. These will change, but so will the PSE. Of course there are more and less challenging, demanding and developed interpretations and better and worse ways of arriving at them, and some of these will be discussed later in the chapter.

Recent developments in primary PSE

In 1988 I wrote:

> Where schools and individual teachers have started to develop conscious policies for PSE, lack of clarity about its nature and purpose has led a number of them to seek the security of a definitive definition of the area.
>
> (Lang 1988: 11)

I went on to suggest that such a definitive definition was probably unachievable and also that it wasn't the end product which was the most important thing. What really mattered was the quality of the thought and discussion that went into establishing what PSE meant in a particular situation. In this chapter I shall be writing from much the same point of view, and my concern will be to encourage the quality of the debate not to provide any universal panaceas. Since writing in 1988 there has not been a great deal of development in terms of thinking or clarification so far as PSE at the primary phase has been concerned, though there have been some useful developments, some of which will be discussed later.

The first book to focus on this area *Thinking About ... Personal and Social Education in the Primary School* (Lang 1988) has undoubtedly been influential, and in the six years since its publication only one other book has appeared which deals specifically with PSE in the primary school. Delwyn and Eva Tattum's (1992) book, though taking a specifically 'symbolic interactionist' approach, does provide an overall approach to a particular version of PSE. The subject has thus been neglected and in some ways the overall situation has become more confused. In 1988 initiatives relating to PSE were found at the level of individual schools and in some cases groups of schools. Apart from this a number of local authorities also produced guidelines. There were however no national policy guidelines. Thus, if there was any encouragement for primary schools it tended to be local. In 1989 the Department of Education and Science (DES) published a pamphlet *Personal and Social Education from 5 to 16* in their 'Curriculum

Matters' series (DES 1989) which presented a view of PSE which matches the one taken in this chapter. It was in 1990 that a significant change occurred. This involved the publication by the National Curriculum Council (NCC) of *Curriculum Guidance Three: The Whole Curriculum* (CG3) (NCC 1990). Here the main emphasis was on the five cross-curricular themes that are considered in other chapters in this book. Not all of these themes had previously been seen as being particularly central to PSE, and this new emphasis has tended to confuse ideas about what PSE in the primary school involves, and also to divert attention from a short section in the document which does give much clearer guidance:

> Clearly the whole curriculum as described in this document contributes to the personal and social education of all pupils. The cross-curricular elements so far described are significant but do not encompass all that is PSE. The themes are concerned with the physical, sexual, moral, social and vocational self but subjects of the national Curriculum, religious education, additional subjects and the extra-curricular activities described in this guidance also play their part. How the curriculum is managed, its organisation and the teaching methods deployed, the unique combination of factors which create the ethos of a school – its aims, attitudes, values and procedures – all make an important contribution to personal and social education programmes in schools.
>
> (NCC 1990: 7)

The section goes on to stress the importance of PSE in preparing young people for their adult roles, and concludes: 'In short the personal and social development of pupils is a major aim of education; personal and social education being the means by which this aim is achieved' (NCC 1990: 7). This short statement is a clear and useful outline of the key factors within schools that influence the personal and social development of pupils and provides a good starting point for the development of the sort of overarching PSE policy to be suggested below. The confusion arises not from what is said, but from the status that it is afforded in the document, which in itself is only concerned with guidance rather than having mandatory status. These points on PSE come at the very end of the first half of the document which deals with the 'whole curriculum', and appear almost as an afterthought. More confusing is the fact that after this point PSE is not mentioned again in any national document or policy, conveying to some the impression that it has been dropped or at least is afforded little importance. In the Office for Standards in Education (OFSTED) *Handbook for the Inspection of Schools*, the area which would normally be associated with PSE has become 'pupils' personal development and behaviour' and is sub-headed 'Spiritual', 'Moral', 'Social' and 'Cultural' (OFSTED 1993: 85). The relationship between these and PSE is not made explicit; indeed there is no specific mention of PSE in the handbook. This could superficially convey the impression to schools that the area does not require development as it will not be inspected. In fact if the 'amplification of evaluation criteria' are consulted it is hard to see how a school could meet the model of effective practice without some form of PSE:

> A school exhibits high standards in these aspects if its work is based on clear principles and values expressed through its aims and evident in its practice. Pupils are encouraged, and show a capacity, to reflect on the experiences of life and to seek explanations for events in the physical and natural world. They are able to discuss their own and other people's beliefs and to understand how these contribute to individual and group identity. In response to opportunities afforded to them, pupils take on and exercise responsibility with maturity, show initiative and seek to extend their social and cultural experiences. Relationships are open and consistent.
>
> (OFSTED 1994: 85)

Again although spiritual and moral development have been highlighted for particular attention in a discussion paper (NCC 1993), and the content has a number of clear connections with PSE, this is not made explicit or reflected upon. Indeed the sudden dropping of the use of the term PSE with no explanation just after it had first appeared as part of the National Curriculum's policy might be thought to be the result of political expediency rather than educational logic.

Whatever the reasons for ignoring the notion of PSE and not making explicit its relationship with the modified terminology of spiritual, moral, social and cultural development, OFSTED and the NCC have inadvertently created confusion which requires considerable effort on the part of schools to resolve. At a time of significant pressure on primary schools it is not surprising that schools which are already uncertain about PSE might give up on it when confronted with the situation outlined above.

PSE in primary schools today

Today, as in 1988, PSE developments in primary schools appear to be very uneven. This was confirmed by a recent small survey undertaken by the author. A sample of 20 primary schools in different parts of England and Northern Ireland responded to questions about the importance they attached to PSE. The questions covered PSE policy and PSE's place in the school development plan, staff support policies, putting PSE into practice in the classroom, whole school policies, cross-curricular themes, and moral, spiritual, social and cultural development. Though the majority of schools attached a degree of importance to all of these areas there were quite considerable differences in those degrees. What was perhaps most significant was some of the comments made, such as: 'All the above areas are of great interest to me. As head of a nursery school, we aim to cover and develop all areas'; 'PSE is part of our development plan'; 'We have a member of staff who is very supportive of members of staff'; 'While I might be aware/interested in PSE other staff are not as yet'; 'Staff attitudes vary a lot'; 'We have no proper policy yet'; 'There is little support from our LEA'. From this it is clear that even where primary schools see themselves as having well developed policies for PSE what this means can vary considerably.

In one school I have visited every class runs circle time sessions. At the beginning of each year the class discusses what rules they might need to work well and happily together, and these are always expressed as positive do's rather than don'ts. These 'golden rules' are written down and signed by everyone (including the teacher) and put up on the wall. These classroom rules are regularly reviewed in the circle. From all of the class rules the head teacher produces a synthesis of six rules which become the school rules for that year. The discipline procedure is laid down as responding with a quiet whisper first; next, the child is taken to one side and the situation discussed, and if this fails the child is set individual work and asked to reflect on how they want their day to be. The final step will be a visit to the head or deputy. A key point is that the discipline procedure, though effective, is carefully devised to try to ensure that pupils do not experience the kind of counterproductive public humiliation sometimes associated with primary discipline. It is also important to note that at this school lunch time assistants are fully involved in the behaviour policy. Parents are also fully involved in what goes on and their cooperation is sought with both the praise and sanction aspects of the policy. This school lays great emphasis on praise but it also uses one form of punishment. On Friday morning the children in each class have what is known as privilege time, which normally lasts for half an hour during which pupils choose from a range of activities which the class has already decided they particularly enjoy doing. Pupils can forfeit privilege time and this normally happens in five-minute blocks. They simply continue to do their class work until privilege time is over and then join in with the others once again. Good behaviour and effort can earn privilege time back. This school has a wide range of ways of encouraging and praising pupils, such as stickers of all kinds, notes to parents and one particularly sensitive form of praise in the form of the secret note. Teachers who see pupils doing something that warrants praise may slip a note into the pupil's pocket which says: 'I was pleased when I saw you. . .'. It is then up to them whom they tell.

By contrast in another school the staff agreed a set of rules:

1 follow instructions the first time;
2 do not stop others from working;
3 keep your hands, feet and objects to yourself;
4 raise your hand before speaking;
5 look after equipment and property.

The school states to parents:

If your children choose to disobey the rules the scale of sanctions on any one day are:
1 name written down (some teachers do this on the board);
2 lose ten minutes playtime;
3 sent to another class to work for 30 minutes;
4 parents contacted;
5 sent to head teacher and kept in isolation;
6 suspension.

This school also stresses praise, the main forms being certificates and telephone calls home. This school perceives this policy as PSE. Parents were simply informed of the policy and were not involved in its development.

An important difference between the policies of the two schools has been their starting point. In the first school there was concern for the nature of relationships throughout the school and the policy was directed at all in the school community. In the second school there was concern about the behaviour of some children and the effect that this was having on the work of the rest, and as a result the policy was directed only at pupils. We will all doubtless favour one or other of these approaches, but in both cases the schools involved believe they are successful in terms of achieving what they set out to do.

Some recent developments

There have been some recent developments which can contribute to effective PSE, and three different examples are set out below. 'Circle time' has already been mentioned and is a technique which has the potential to be developed into a whole school policy as in the case of the school discussed earlier. Alternatively it may simply be used in individual classrooms two or three times a week or when the teacher or pupils feel it is needed. Writers such as White (1991, 1992) and Mosley (1993) argue that circle time can make a significant contribution to PSE, particularly in terms of enhancing pupil self-esteem. Circle time can be used for problem solving, creating shared rules, planning, developing the ability to talk about feelings and, importantly, the skills of basic empathy, understanding and respecting the feelings of others. The rules for the most basic form of circle time are that everyone sits in the circle and is at the same level. An object is passed round the circle when you are holding it and it is your turn to talk, though no one has to talk who doesn't want to. When someone is talking everyone else listens and negative statements about others in the circle are unacceptable. A key point is that the teacher follows the same rules as the pupils.

While circle time provides a process through which PSE can be delivered, *Skills for the Primary School Child* (The Advisory Council on Alcohol and Drug Education (TACADE) 1993) can provide a programme. The package includes a manual, workshops for schools and for parents, and a set of lesson cards. The lesson cards are divided into six sections with five lessons in each. The titles of the sections are:

• Me a special person
• One of many
• Feelings and emotions
• Learning new skills
• Facing challenges
• Looking after myself.

Skills for the Primary School Child can form a useful part of a wider approach to PSE but is less successful if seen in terms of the whole approach.

Process and programme are important but unless they are underpinned by a view of what is being sought they may end up as aimless and mere routine. The Hertfordshire Local Education Authority guidelines offer one suggestion on the way attention may be focused on the actual objectives of PSE:

> One way of achieving a 'whole person approach' to PSE is described by Watkins (1992) as the 'seven selves' which he has adapted from a concept devised by Wall in 1947. The list he uses is:
> • bodily self
> • sexual self
> • social self
> • vocational self
> • moral/political self
> – and, because we are considering the school context,
> • self as learner
> • self in the organisation.
> Using the seven selves is one way of ensuring coverage of the whole curriculum whilst maintaining an approach which arises out of the needs of the individual.
> (Hertfordshire County Council Education Department 1993: 6)

Such a model can be used either as the basis for an overall approach or simply as a means of reflecting on and reviewing an existing policy, and it is to the situation regarding policies that this chapter now turns.

PSE policy development in the primary school

Policies operate in two related but distinct ways; they are a way of checking and if necessary modifying existing documentation and practice, and they are also developed to ensure that a particular range of things happen within the school. In what follows it is the second purpose that is emphasized.

Recently there has been considerable pressure on primary schools to produce policies on a number of affective areas. They have been required to produce policies on sex education and various scandals and reports have created pressure for child protection and bullying policies. Staff concern has also often provided the motivation for the development of a discipline or behaviour policy. A number of primary schools, having developed these policies, have felt it logical to produce a PSE policy to go alongside them. Not surprisingly the level to which these policies are developed varies considerably. An example may be provided by considering the sex education policies in one local authority. At one extreme these include policies which were so short and bland that they provided no guidance in terms of what teachers were actually meant to do at all:

> This is an important part of the school's policy on Health and Safety. However it must be seen in terms of a partnership with parents, who have their own important role to play. At school sex education is taught incidentally as part of other activities or experiences. Questions are dealt with factually and honestly as they arise. Answers are presented in the context of a caring, loving, respectful family. Television programmes, film strips and annual talks by the health visitor may also be used.

Other policies are very well developed, such as one which runs to three and a half pages and whose introduction includes:

> Sex education concerns itself with the whole person and with interpersonal relationships. Sex education comes under the wider umbrella of health, personal, social and moral education, therefore it will encompass the exploration of feelings about love, friendship, fears, trust, respect and responsibility towards self and others. Sex education is not just about biology and how the reproductive system works.

Sex education consists not just of knowledge but of skills and attitudes. Biological facts will be imparted but they will not be divorced from the emotional and practical needs of the child.

The policy goes on to consider the role of parents, the aims of sex education, how it will be taught, topics for ages 4–5, 6–7, 8–9, 10–11, and finally the implications of the National Curriculum for science. The document concludes:

It is envisaged that the content of the sex education programme will adopt the spiral concept of education in that subjects and themes will be repeated from year to year in greater depth using different approaches as pupils mature.

The second policy provides an excellent model both in terms of its development and in the way it locates sex education within the wider bounds of health, personal, social and moral education. Indeed such a policy would fit well into the overarching approach to PSE to be discussed below.

Developing an overarching PSE policy

Whatever their quality, the provision of a number of fragmentary PSE related policies provide not only the least challenging approach but also the least effective. The alternative, which is both the more challenging and the more effective, is to produce an overarching PSE policy which includes and synthesizes all the other related policies. Such an approach to policy allows for the sort of integration I have argued for in relation to counselling in primary schools (Lang 1993). Such a policy would not only address the broad issues of whole school climate and ethos but incorporate bullying and behaviour policies, health, sex education and child protection, race and gender equality and all of the other curricular and cross-curricular themes and dimensions.

In the end policies are significant not for what is written down but for what actually happens. This is not as some schools believe a reason for taking things for granted and not bothering to write anything at all. The point is that in thinking about and developing an overarching policy, the way that what is being discussed and recorded relates to what happens must be part of the process from the start. There is little point in producing long lists of the personal qualities that are seen as desirable in pupils if the means by which they might be promoted is not also being reflected upon.

An overarching PSE policy should be developed by paying equal attention to the starting point and the point of delivery. The policy should start from some form of shared values and its final articulation should ensure that it reaches all aspects of the school's life and work.

How should such a policy be best developed and sustained? I believe that there are a number of key elements to achieving this. Schools need to start from a set of common values which are reviewed on a regular basis. It is only when a school is clear on these that it can establish what PSE should mean in its specific case. These values need in part to stem from some form of needs analysis and be translated into a set of aims. From these aims policies are developed and the processes through which these will actually operate considered. Provision should be made for reflection at an individual and institutional level, and finally, ways in which the policy will be maintained and evaluated must be established.

Needs, values and aims

It would be surprising if schools did not recognize many of the needs of their pupils, but often there are things that are missed. They need to approach the assessment of their pupils' needs in a reflective way, to discuss these needs, and base their conclusions on as much hard data as possible. There is a tendency to oversimplify or stereotype the needs that a school's pupils have. Schools need to challenge the basis of this and question its validity. Having clarified its view of its pupils' needs a school is confronted with an even more important task, one which will partly reflect the needs it has identified. This is the discussion of the values that should underpin the school's work. Schools need to devote both time and preparation to this, as the aim is to end with a set of core values that everyone in the school understands and can support. In this way the problems identified by Galloway quoted earlier can be avoided. Though such a process does not guarantee the successful development of aims and policies it certainly gives a much better chance of such a development than when the starting point is taken for granted and involves untested assumptions. Common values have to be translated into aims and aims into policies. The ideal situation is where all of those making up the school and community partnership are involved. At the very least all the staff should play an active part, and at best all the children and their parents will also be involved.

Maintenance

From the start it is essential to remember that an effective policy needs more than just effective ways of putting it into practice. Agreeing to something and providing teachers with the skills to put it into practice is an essential start but not enough to ensure that it endures. For something to endure thought needs to be given to what I describe as 'maintenance'; the ways in which a school plans to keep its policies vital, active, responsive and evolving. Three important parts of this are reflection, review and evaluation. Reflection should operate at two levels; that of the individual and that of the institution. Ideally all staff should be given the opportunity to talk about their practice and their feelings about it on an individual basis. Clearly such opportunities will be difficult to provide regularly but one way this might be done is through the use of circle time, which would allow every member of staff to share their feelings. It is also important for schools as a whole to provide a regular space to reflect on the operation and effectiveness of their policies. One school I have visited has set aside one staff meeting a month to reflect on how they are progressing on 'their journey' as they choose to express it. Closely linked with the idea of reflection are those of review and evaluation, and clearly the process of reflection will be informed by both of these. Again, both will need to be planned for. Review involves either looking in a general way at the overall picture of how things are going, or focusing on a specific aspect. Evaluation can support this or be undertaken separately, the key difference being that it will involve the use of specific techniques and/or instruments in measuring the outcomes of the PSE policy or aspects of it. Schools need to return to the common values they agreed and spend time reflecting on whether these still remain appropriate to their current situation. One village primary school has done just this. Values agreed in 1989 were reviewed in 1993 and as the staff felt the school had made considerable progress in the four years their statement of values was modified and substantially recast.

Conclusion

If seen as a simple bolt-on programme of predetermined activities PSE is unlikely to engage pupils in any significant way, and where it is left to chance and general good intentions a great deal is likely to be neglected. Not only is PSE an intentional activity it is also central to a wide range of current primary school concerns and to aspects of their curriculums. It has been argued that if appropriate policies and effective practice are to be developed it is the more challenging approaches which need to be chosen. The development of effective PSE in the primary school should involve a journey where, though some of the destinations may be clear, much is initially uncertain, and such a journey requires effort and reflection if it is to succeed. In this chapter I have not sought to provide any ready-made solution, indeed there can be none, as the first and most important step is for the individual school to recognize the importance of PSE for itself. This does not usually happen solely as the result of reading a book or because of external pressure. My concern has been to suggest ways in which schools can begin to make sense of what remains a confused situation. I have stressed that in the end the way in which PSE is interpreted depends on the individual school, but I have also argued that there are a number of general principles that characterize it. I have outlined what I believe to be the essential steps that schools must take to convert a recognition of the need for PSE into effective policy and practice.

Perhaps the most difficult but equally most important thing for schools to recognize is that the development of effective PSE in the primary school depends just as much on the quality of the journey as the importance of the destination.

References

Department of Education and Science (DES)/Her Majesty's Inspectorate (HMI) (1980) *A View of the Curriculum*. London: HMSO.

Department of Education and Science (DES) (1989) *Personal and Social Education from 5 to 16*, Curriculum Matters 14: an HMI series. London: HMSO.

Galloway, D. (1990) *Pupil Welfare and Counselling: an Approach to Personal and Social Education Across the Curriculum*. London: Longman.

Hertfordshire County Council Education Department (1993) *Personal, Social and Health Education (PSHE) in the Primary Phase*. Hertford: Hertfordshire County Council.

Lang, P. (1988) Introduction, in P. Lang (ed.) *Thinking About . . . Personal and Social Education in the Primary School*. Oxford: Basil Blackwell.

Lang, P. (1993) Counselling in the primary school: an integrated approach, in K. Bovair and C. McLaughlin (eds) *Counselling in Schools: A Reader*. London: David Fulton Publishers.

Mosley, J. (1993) *Turn Your School Round*. Wisbech: LDA.

National Curriculum Council (NCC) (1990) *Curriculum Guidance Three: The Whole Curriculum*. York: NCC.

National Curriculum Council (NCC) (1993) *Spiritual and Moral Development: a Discussion Paper*. York: NCC.

Office for Standards in Education (OFSTED) (1993) *Handbook for the Inspection of Schools*. London: HMSO.

Office for Standards in Education (OFSTED) (1994) *Handbook for the Inspection of Schools, May amendment*. London: HMSO.

The Advisory Council on Alcohol and Drug Education (TACADE) (1993) (second edition) *Skills for the Primary School Child: Promoting the Protection of Children*. Salford: TACADE.

Tattum, D. and Tattum, E. (1992) *Social Education and Personal Development*. London: David Fulton Publishers.

Watkins, C. (1992) *Whole School PSE: Policy and Practice*. Warwick: NAPCE.

White, M. (1991) *Self-Esteem: Promoting Positive Practice for Responsible Behaviour; Circle Time Strategies for Schools, Set A.* Cambridge: Daniels Publishing.

White, M. (1992) *Self-Esteem: Its Meaning, and Value In Schools: How to Help Children Learn Readily and Behave Well, Set B.* Cambridge: Daniels Publishing.

Index

SPECIAL EDUCATIONAL NEEDS IN THE PRIMARY SCHOOL
A PRACTICAL GUIDE

Jean Gross

Local management of schools and cutbacks in central support services mean that the responsibility for meeting special educational needs is resting ever more squarely on the shoulders of ordinary classroom teachers. Yet few feel wholly confident in their ability to adapt work within the national curriculum to meet the whole range of needs, or coordinate successful action plans for children who – for whatever reason – are not learning as well as they might.

This book will increase that confidence. Aimed at busy class teachers, special needs coordinators, heads and teachers in training, it shows how the teacher can build differentiation into planning lessons and schemes of work. It describes workable strategies for managing the most common behaviour difficulties and meeting special needs in language and mathematics.

At a whole school level, it offers practical guidance on developing special needs policies, assessment, record keeping, and the management of time, roles and resources. The focus is on the ways in which schools can do a good job in meeting special needs themselves, within everyday constraints of time, money and energy, and in doing so hold back the tide of increasing marginalization of vulnerable children within the education system.

Contents
Current perspectives on special educational needs – Developing a whole school policy – Special needs and the national curriculum – Assessment and special educational needs – Action planning and record keeping – Managing time – Managing roles and resources – Managing behaviour – Communication and classroom relationships – Special needs in speaking and listening – Special needs in reading – Special needs in writing – Special needs in maths – Beyond the school – References – Index.

240pp   0 335 19035 9 (Paperback)

CREATIVE TEACHERS IN PRIMARY SCHOOLS

Peter Woods

Is creative teaching still possible in English schools? Can teachers maintain and promote their own interests and beliefs as well as deliver a prescribed National Curriculum?

This book explores creative teachers' attempts to pursue *their* brand of teaching despite the changes. Peter Woods has discovered a range of strategies and adaptations to this end among such teachers, including resisting change which runs counter to their own values; appropriating the National Curriculum within their own ethos; enhancing their role through the use of others; and enriching their work through the National Curriculum to provide quality learning experiences. If all else fails, such teachers remove themselves from the system and take their creativity elsewhere. A strong theme of self-determination runs through these experiences.

While acknowledging hard realities, the book is ultimately optimistic, and a tribute to the dedication and inspiration of primary teachers.

The book makes an important contribution to educational theory, showing a range of responses to intensification as well as providing many detailed examples of collaborative research methods.

Contents
Introduction: Adapting to intensification – Resisting through collaboration: A whole-school perspective of the National Curriculum – The creative use and defence of space: Appropriation through the environment – The charisma of the critical other: Enhancing the role of the teacher – Teaching, and researching the teaching of, a history topic: An experiment in collaboration – Managing marginality: Aspects of the career of a primary school head – Self-determination among primary school teachers – References – Index.

208pp   0 335 19313 7 (paperback)   0 335 19314 5 (Hardback)

ORGANIZING FOR LEARNING IN THE PRIMARY CLASSROOM
A BALANCED APPROACH TO CLASSROOM MANAGEMENT

Janet R. Moyles

What is it that underlies classroom organization, routines, rules, structures and daily occurrences? What are the prime objectives and what influences the decisions of teachers and children? What is it useful for teachers to consider when contemplating the issues of classroom management and organization? What do different practices have to offer?

Organizing for Learning in the Primary Classroom explores the whole range of influences and values which underpin *why* teachers do *what* they do in the classroom context and what these mean to children and others. Janet Moyles examines teaching and learning styles, children's independence and autonomy, coping with children's differences, the physical classroom context and resources, time management and ways of involving others in the day-to-day organization. Practical suggestions are given for considering both the functional and aesthetic aspects of the classroom context. Opportunities are provided for teachers to reflect on their own organization and also consider innovative and flexible ways forward to deal with new and ever-increasing demands on their time and sanity!

This book is to be highly recommended for all primary school teachers . . .
(Management in Education)

. . . indispensable to courses in initial teacher education and to providers of inset.

(Child Education)

Janet Moyles brings her long experience of the primary school to *Organizing for Learning in the Primary Classroom* . . . I particularly like the attention she gives to the physical environment, giving lots of advice about arrangements of furniture and the role of the teacher's desk . . .
(The Times Educational Supplement)

Contents

Introduction: Polarizations and balance – Teachers and teaching: beliefs and values – The learning environment: organizing the classroom context – The children and their learning needs: balancing individual and whole class approaches – Grouping children for teaching and learning: providing equal opportunities and promoting appropriate behaviour – Time for teaching and learning – Deploying adult help effectively in the classroom: delegation and responsibility – Evaluating classroom organization and management – Conclusion: the primary classroom, a place and a time – References – Index.

208pp   0 335 15659 2 (Paperback)   0 335 15660 6 (Hardback)